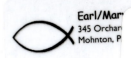

THERE IS MUCH
RUBBISH

Follow Nehemiah on a journey
to rebuild your life.

Earl —
Build the Wall!
Out with the rubbish.
Stephen Stutzman

STEVE STUTZMAN
from Stutzman Family Singers

Copyright 2020 by
Steve Stutzman
Strait Paths Foundation
P.O. Box 176
Ronks, PA 17572

All rights reserved. No part of this publication may be reproduced in any form without written permission from the publisher, except in the case of documented quotations for research and reviews.

ISBN: 978-0-9910171-4-0

Cover Design by: Meg Delagrange

Printed by
Schlabach Printers
798 SR 93 NW, Sugarcreek OH 44681
330.852.4687

Contents

Note to the Reader 2

Much Rubbish 3

Babylon 8

Excursus 15

Estimated at Time of Return Trek 18

The Trek 19

Foundations 25

Resistance 32

Temple 40

Unprotected 49

Building the Wall 57

Uncovering Foundation 67

Repentance 79

Dominion 92

Journey to Effective Kingdom Authority 101

Jerusalem 103

Note to the Reader

This book needs to be read with an awareness that there are several layers of meaning to be understood. First, there's a fictional narrative based on real Bible characters named in Ezra and Nehemiah. Second, as those characters return from exile in Babylon to their ancestral home of Jerusalem and rebuild the temple and the city walls, their lives are impacted by unseen spiritual realities. And finally, from the experiences of the characters in the story, the author makes applications to our lives in the 21st century.

The first layer is simply an enjoyable read that invites you to imagine some of the emotions experienced by the returning exiles. The second (and even more the third) layers of meaning are largely allegorical, and it will be helpful to keep that fact in mind as you read. When the author challenges you to "build a temple in your life," he's not suggesting that you head to your local lumberyard for supplies to build an actual structure in your backyard. When he warns you against "renting out a room in the temple," he's referring to a literal event in the story with a spiritual warning against getting friendly with the enemy.

If an allusion to a spiritual application from the story doesn't make sense to you at first, just keep reading. It all becomes clear as the story progresses, and you will discover that Johanan's experience is full of lessons, warnings, and instructions for followers of Jesus today.

Editor
Andrew Weaver

This book is not a novel. It is an intentional look deep into our own souls, concerning who we are, why we are, and where we are. It is intended for those who want more, but are uncertain how to proceed. It will require of you intentional attention, and time for elements in consciousness to shift. May God give you revelation as you read.

Stephen Stutzman

> **It is difficult to find worth, or meaning, until the heart has found rest.** -SS

CHAPTER 1

Much Rubbish

The small boy lifted his pack and adjusted it on his back. He took one last drink from the flask, knowing it would be a long, hot day. As if on cue, Zerubbabel emerged from the trees on horseback and sounded the trumpet. The day had begun. Johanan began walking. It was, in many ways, like the day before and the day after. Men and boys laden with packs, youths herding animals on foot and on horseback, long lines of camels swaying rhythmically under their loads, crowds of women and children shuffling, and ox carts creaking. There were over 50,000 souls in all, traveling 750 miles across deserts on the east side of Israel, in areas we know today as Syria and Iraq.

The year was 486 BC. Cyrus, King of Persia, had given the order for Jews to be returned to the land of Israel and its capital city, Jerusalem. There, he instructed, they were to build a house, a temple to the Lord God of heaven. This appears to be some 40 years after the city had been destroyed and the temple razed by Nebuchadnezzar, king of Babylon.

King Belshazzar of Babylon, after the party scene where a hand appeared writing on the wall, had been overthrown. On the night of the party, a king named Cyrus from 300 miles east had overthrown the city and usurped the throne. For whatever reason, Cyrus revered God, and one of his first acts was to send the Israelites back to their native land. He then returned to Shushan and left Darius as king in Babylon. This is the same Darius who appears in the story of Daniel in the lions' den.

It is possible, though not at all certain, that King Cyrus was present at the fiery furnace years earlier when the three Hebrews, Shadrach, Meshach, and Abednego, refused to bow and worship Nebuchadnezzar's golden image. If so, it certainly would explain his concern that the REAL God of heaven have His house built.

In any event, the crowd of 50,000 migrants moved slowly westward. They were headed home. More than that, they were headed to the land of their fathers, a land promised to them by God Himself. But most importantly, they were headed home to build a temple. It would be a temple to God, THE temple to God, the only one on the planet, to establish some connection once again with a God Who had been rejected.

For the people had rejected their God. Not intentionally, perhaps, but still, it had happened. Laws were rejected, sabbaths forsaken, and prophets ignored. Consequently, the city was destroyed, people were either enslaved or killed, the temple was razed, and the gold was carried off with the slaves. For 40 years they suffered the yoke of bondage, and now were headed home again.

I weep when I read the story. Jeremiah wept when he saw it coming. He marveled that no one saw or cared, and wept until his eyes were as fountains.

Is it nothing to you, all ye that pass by? Behold and see if there be any sorrow like unto my sorrow, which is done unto me, wherewith the Lord hath afflicted me in the day of his fierce anger. (Lamentation 1:12)

> *Oh, that my head were waters, and mine eyes a fountain of tears, that I might weep day and night for the slain of the daughter of my people! (Jeremiah 9:1)*

His torment of soul is recorded in a book of lament that we call Lamentations. It is a lament for the pain, the death, the horror, the rape, and the destruction. It is a lament for a people torn from their land, their hope, their community, and their society. More than that, it is a lament for the rejection of God, the forsaking of His ways, and the avoidable, needless nature of it all. Yet deeper still, in the recesses of the heart, was pain of spirit; pain that His God should be blasphemed.

> *When that which should be glory is turned to mockery and shame, the spirit of the prophet is wounded.*

In the Mideastern mindset, it was not the best army or general who won battles. It was clearly the side with the best god. That's why David approached Goliath in the name of his God. It is why the Midianites were terrified of Gideon. It is why the Canaanites feared Israel. And . . . it is why Jerusalem remained cocky, even when surrounded by Nebuchadnezzar and his armies. But Jeremiah knew. He knew that this time, God wasn't going to move to save Jerusalem. And he knew why; because God and His ways had been rejected.

> ***If so be they will hearken, and turn every man from his evil way, that I may repent me of the evil, which I purpose to do unto them because of the evil of their doings. (Jeremiah 26:3)***

Individuals like Daniel also knew. Even after his family was killed and his city destroyed, he resolutely knelt by an open window and faced toward Jerusalem to pray. Three times a day, he openly declared his allegiance to a city now fallen and a God dishonored. Without any record of being commanded to do so, he persisted, even if it meant being thrown to ravenous lions. May God find men of this caliber today, men who are committed to what is absolute and right, and not simply to what seems expedient.

The purpose of this book is not to tell a story. Rather, it is to apply a storyline in our lives. We want to extrapolate from the given story that which is directly pictured in our own lives. Gods people, called by His name, had fallen into a serious state of disobedience. Because of this, they were taken into bondage to a foreign king. The people did not place high enough priority on God or on keeping His commands. This brought them into servitude.

Let me be clear here, I am writing to the people of God, Christians if you will, who wake up one day and find themselves trapped. Far from home under a foreign king of sin and selfishness, or perhaps a vicious king of control or performance, we sigh. The joy is gone. Shame and confusion are on every side, and even our very identity hangs in question. Loud screams and stinging lashes are the only reality we know. Then one of our slave drivers—our lust, our shame, our fear—comes to us and says, "Sing! Sing a song of Zion!"

> **By the rivers of Babylon, there we sat down, yea, we wept, when we remembered Zion. We hanged our harps upon the willows in the midst thereof. For there they that carried us away captive required of us a song; and they that wasted us required of us mirth, saying, Sing us one of the songs of Zion. How shall we sing the Lord's song in a strange land? (Psalm 137:1-4)**

Forty years is long enough. God wants to bring you again into a land of milk and honey, a place of sustenance and sweetness. He wants to bring back your song. He wants the altar built again in you, where sacrifices of praise will be offered daily. He wants to be your Lord, your King, your Friend, and your Brother.

It may be a long journey. It might be a bit hot and dry on the road home, but here is the reality you must grapple with: **YOU DON'T BELONG HERE.** You weren't made for slavery and joyless servitude.

> **You do not belong in a place of slavery and servitude. You were designed for much more than this.**

So, the first order of business is a temple. God wants a temple; a place to abide, a place to meet, an avenue through which to influence the world. That temple, my friend, is you. That city, Jerusalem? It is your life.

So ... you will need to go back to your life. It will be hard work to build a temple. Enemies will threaten and harass you. Your former king will try to stop you. And then, after the temple is done, you will build the WALL. All hell will come against you then, but you must get to the foundation, the solid, core realities that never moved. You will have to move piles of debris to uncover the foundations and understand the original design.

It will be dangerous. You will be attacked. The work will be extremely hard and the conditions brutal. You will endure personal wounding, blisters, and damage. You will live with the scars of it all.

But the greatest problem of all? **THERE WAS MUCH RUBBISH.**

Q. Daniel experienced a horrible event that could have made him wounded and bitter. Instead, he focused in on his God. What events in your life might have obscured the reality of God to you?

_____

_____

_____

_____

Q. What specific things do the most damage to the "song" in your life?

_____

_____

_____

_____

Q. What do you see as rubbish in your life now?

_____

_____

_____

_____

10   Much Rubbish

> Man, on his own, seeking to find God, will always create an oppressive Babylon. -SS

CHAPTER 2

Babylon

Johanan yawned and stretched, then rolled off his cot. Father Eliashib had called ,and another day was begun.

Another grey day, Johanan mused. One day just melted away, and turned into the next. Life didn't hold a lot of meaning, or promise, here in Babylon. Johanan's entire people group was mostly despised, and being a minority here meant daily scoffing and rude gestures. He had friends of course, but even together they were sometimes mocked as odd.

Eliashib mostly just kept his head down and went about his business. Eliashib was born in Babylon, and this captivity was all he knew of life.

Well, almost all.

Great Grandpa Jeshua came over some nights to tell stories. Johanan loved to hear them, there was something so very comforting, and soothing about them. There was a quiet, subdued yearning in Jeshua's voice, that spoke to a deep spot in Johanan's heart that he couldn't explain. But in general, life in Babylon had a very same-old, same-old feeling. There was very little of purpose or desire in life.

"We don't belong here" Great grandpa Jeshua often muttered. "We belong in a land given to us by God, to our Father Abraham."

Johana came in off the street that evening, and immediately felt the difference. The air was electric. Father, Grandpa, and great-grandpa were talking animatedly in the next room. Johanan looked at his mother, preparing the evening meal. Her eyes brimmed with tears and her face spoke both hope and pain. Johanan's mind spun with questions.

The men finally emerged from the room, and gathered to eat. Rabbi Ezra was also with them, and even though they seemed serious, there was an energized expectancy that emanated from the men. Johanan looked quizzically at his father.

The men spoke thanks to God for the food, and began to eat. Then Jeshua spoke, quietly and resolutely. "We are going to leave Babylon. We are going to Jerusalem.

Babylon has an interesting history. It seems that a tribal mentality took over an early group of people. Concerned lest they be scattered from their tribe, they built a city and a tower called Babel.

And they said, Go to, let us build us a city and a tower, whose top may reach unto heaven; and let us make us a name, lest we be scattered abroad upon the face of the whole earth. (Genesis 11:4)

God came down to watch and was not very impressed. He sent a division of language, turning the organization of Babel into the disorganization of babble. This organized disorder became a symbol of the enemy of God's city, Jerusalem.

Therefore is the name of it called Babel; because the Lord did there confound the language of all the earth: and from thence did the Lord scatter them abroad upon the face of all the earth. (Genesis 11:9)

The desire people have to reach God seems so very right, good, and noble. However, when coupled with the earthly elements of man's desire, the entire enterprise becomes hijacked. Mixing the mud of human design with the straw of human desire will never produce a building material suitable for a habitation of God. (Genesis 11:3)

The effort of man to produce heat to fire bricks is still man's idea. And if you look closely, you will see in Genesis the desire of man for a NAME. There is something of control, "lest we be scattered'" that speaks of safety to man's heart and gives him identity. Somehow people feel safer when crowded together. Well over half the population of the world lives crowded in cities, while in the United States, the rate is more like 80%.

This effort of man to bring order, to feel safe, to create a tribe, and to reach God on human terms has been the curse on religion ever since. The efforts to turn LIFE into a system create entities that inadvertently set themselves up against God. A look into history reveals the development of religions all over the earth: Buddhism, Hinduism, Islam, and tribal religions around the globe. Closer to home, many folks are born into a Christian religious system that has been built in a similar fashion.

God brought in an answer: babble. One person spoke, but another could not understand. Slowly, people congregated around their group, the ones who spoke the same language and understood one another. This became their tribe. Babel, the city that started it all, became known as Babylon. It stands throughout time as a nemesis to God's city and Satan's perversion of the same. And it was this city that held Jerusalem hostage.

Not a lot has changed. Even today, people journeying across the sand of time stop to build a structure of safety to bring them identity.

Unless this is done carefully, the end result will always be another Babylon. Many of us were born into these kinds of systems or came upon them in our own journeys. There is a certain sameness about them, an effort to bring about human control. Perimeters with insiders/outsiders, some sort of tower intended to reach heaven, and confusion of communications that brings separations and division.

The towers vary a lot, but they all hold the same promise of keeping folks together while reaching heaven. There are towers of lifestyles, communions, activities, soul-winning, giftings, class, race, families, tongues, worship days, beliefs, viewpoints, buggies, worship styles, backgrounds...and the list could continue. It is not so much that any of these things are wrong in and of themselves. Rather, it is turning them into a "tower that reaches to heaven" that allows the entire city to become a tool of the enemy against God's people. Eventually, this Babylon system brings God's people into captivity, and they struggle to return to Jerusalem.

Babylon always comes against the free people of God.

Babylon comes against the free people of God. Prophets cry warnings, begging for folks to repent. They are hushed and thrown into pits. Babylon destroys the outer edges that provide sustenance: the vineyards of joy, the wheat fields of victory, the olive trees of worship, the lentils of obedience, and the gardens of humility. Spiritual food becomes scarce. Then walls are torn down, houses burned, and even the temple destroyed. Many people are devastated and never recover. The choicest, most obedient men are mutilated and taken to Babylon to serve the system.

Please understand that I am not against you. It is not your tribe I despise, or your particular tower or family tree that I hate. It is for Jerusalem that my heart bleeds. As says the songwriter,

For her my tears shall fall,
For her my prayer ascend;
To her my cares and toils be given,
Till toils and cares shall end.

Beyond my highest joys
I prize her heavenly ways,
Her sweet communion, solemn vows,
Her hymns of joy and praise.

(Timothy Dwight, grandson of Jonathan Edwards, President of Yale)

I seek the rebuilding of the temple, the reality of Christ dwelling in us, the worship, and the holy presence. As David so aptly said after the ark of the covenant was removed from the tabernacle for 40 years:

> **One thing have I desired of the Lord, that will I seek after; that I may dwell in the house of the Lord all the days of my life, to behold the beauty of the Lord, and to enquire in his temple. (Psalms 27:4)**

Some who live in these Babylons never forget. They remember Jerusalem. They refuse the defilement, and although they serve a foreign king, their allegiance is always toward Jerusalem. They look for the opportunity to portray the superiority of the real God of heaven to the Babel system. Sometimes, as with Daniel and his friends, these opportunities come at great personal risk. And sometimes they cause whole systems of Babylon to temporarily halt and shift toward the God of Jerusalem.

Somewhere in the midst of Babylon, somewhere amongst the organized chaos of systems, stands a Daniel. Alone, and even serving a foreign king, a Daniel never forgets his God. He never forgets who he is, Whom he belongs to, and Who is, finally, God. He chooses to not only align with his God but also to do what is not commanded, simply because he believes his God sees. Against all propriety, against all expediency, Daniel kneels three times a day toward Jerusalem. If you happen to see him, honor him for that stand.

When all is said and done, Babel is still Babylon. Faithful as Daniel and his friends were, Babylon is not Jerusalem. And somewhere, in the midst of those held captive by Babylonish systems, an Ezekiel hears the cry of a living God to His people. He weeps by the river Chebar, seeing visions of things he cannot understand. Still, he takes his assignment seriously and cries out against the evil.

And go, get thee to them of the captivity, unto the children of thy people, and speak unto them, and tell them, Thus saith the Lord God; whether they will hear, or whether they will forbear ... Then I came to them of the captivity at Telabib, that dwelt by the river of Chebar, and I sat where they sat, and remained there astonished among them seven days. And it came to pass at the end of seven days, that the word of the Lord came unto me, saying, Son of man, I have made thee a watchman unto the house of Israel: therefore hear the word at my mouth, and give them warning from me. (Ezekiel 3:11, 15-17)

Some become comfortable in the foreign city. Some never do leave. Some are born into captivity, see it as normal, and regard Ezekiel as a bother. Some have no memory or knowledge of Jerusalem, the city of God. Some of those in captivity cannot understand the burning of hearts in those who MUST return. The edifice of Babel towers over the city, a memorial claiming that because of OUR tower, we are better than others.

You may be wondering right now, wait, is this written to ME? Am I in Babylon? How do I know if my city (life) is Jerusalem (city of God and worship) or if it is Babylon (system of man's control)?

First, scan the horizon of your life and see if there is a tower. What is it in your life that makes you better than others? What is it that brings identity to your tribe? What reaches to heaven for you?

What is it that makes you feel superior to others? That thing is a tower in your Babel.

There is a distinct drive in all mankind to feel better than others. Something in us wants to feel superior, by SOME measure. It might be by symbols, buildings, lifestyle, work ethic, education, popularity, clothing style, worship style, specific doctrine, social issue, race, or any combination of the above. I am not even saying it is bad; it may be a very good thing. BUT . . . if it has created a tribe and has you feeling superior to others, it is a Tower of Babel. It will bring you into Babylon unless you repent. This repentance doesn't mean you stop DOING the good thing. Rather, it means you repent of making the good thing an idol. That Nebuchadnezzar-like drive to be lifted up and somehow feel superior leads to eating grass like an ox. (Daniel 4:33)

I am urging you, church, to examine your heart carefully on this matter. Do you feel superior to other races? Has your community become a tower? Does your language communicate equality to those around you? What are you doing that secretly makes you feel superior to others? Building a big business? Does capitulating to a godless culture make you feel superior to more separated groups? God is looking for a group of people to return to Jerusalem. These will build a temple and later rebuild walls. These are the ones who will restore worship, establish clear lives, and walk in the glory of the King.

This journey to restoration is going to require several things, elements not everyone has or even seeks:

- A reverence for the God of Jerusalem
- A willingness to thoroughly repent with point-blank honesty
- A significant disgust for Babylon
- A love for the laws and ways of God
- A willingness to suffer; guts and determination
- A mind to work
- A vision

Many folks will love conversations about going back to Jerusalem. Ideas of how to accomplish it will abound. But unless there is a deep drive within, a reverence for a holy God, a cry of His Spirit, and honesty that seeks repentance, the whole endeavor will falter. Halfway back, some city in a green valley will beckon. Without a vision, without a love for the God of Jerusalem and His ways, people will park in those places. Disgust for Babylon is not enough. In those cities, people of God will learn to do like the nations about them. They will concede to their ways and eventually to their gods. It is an easier life, to be sure—if you have no mind to work.

God noted sadly that He had been unable to find a man to stand in the gap to prevent the destruction of Israel.

> ***And I sought for a man among them, that should make up the hedge, and stand in the gap before me for the land, that I should not destroy it: but I found none.. (Ezekiel 22:30)***

Now, in a foreign land, such a man was finally found. Daniel lay on his face and wept and fasted, mourning for three full weeks. He recognized the sin that had landed them all in this predicament, and he confessed it. Not only did he confess his sins, but he also confessed sins he didn't even commit, the sins of his people. And he saw why there was confusion:

O Lord, righteousness belongeth unto thee, but unto us confusion of faces, as at this day; to the men of Judah, and to the inhabitants of Jerusalem, and unto all Israel, that are near, and that are far off, through all the countries whither thou hast driven them, because of their trespass that they have trespassed against thee. (Daniel 9:7)

Babylon is not your calling, your destiny, or your destination. You have no inheritance there. Come, let us go unto the mount of our God.

Q. What do you see as "Babylons" around you?

_____
_____
_____
_____
_____

Q. Do any of them have a hold on you?

_____
_____
_____
_____
_____

Q. A common theme of man is trying to look better than others. What would you say is the place this desire rears its head in you?

_____
_____
_____
_____
_____

Excursus

The Bible as it is written is too often examined as if it were a piece of meat. We pore over words, translations, cross-references, and historical context. While I am certainly not against scholarly disciplines, I think we too often shortchange the beauty and glory of its DEPTH.

I love snorkeling. There is that moment off the coast of Belize where you adjust the goggles and plunge into the water. As you descend below the surface of the Caribbean blue, an entire world opens up in front of your eyes. Brightly colored fish, lobsters, seashells, and coral glimmer in the sun as a turtle paddles by. As long as one sits in the boat, only the surface is obvious. But put on glasses and fins, dive in, and an entire world of splendor will leave you in a suspended state of timeless wonder.

For the word of God is quick, and powerful, and sharper than any twoedged sword, piercing even to the dividing asunder of soul and spirit, and of the joints and marrow, and is a discerner of the thoughts and intents of the heart. (Hebrews 4:12)

Such is the Word. While away some time on the surface if you must, but very little of glory and splendor is there. Argue about words, language, translations, and context, but in the end, one will always arrive at a place of frustration when seeking to make ETERNAL truth subject to MORTAL mind. This is an exercise in futility.

Thomas Aquinas was a brilliant scholar in the 13th century. He studied at the University of Paris and taught thousands of hours of lectures. Well versed in philosophy, he wrote extensively on many subjects and is regarded by many to be the single most influential writer of the pre-Reformation church era. Deeply religious, very disciplined, and highly informed and intelligent, Thomas set about to write *Summa Theologiae*, or *Sum of All Theology* before he was even 50 years old. This he did by dictation to multiple secretaries simultaneously.

But one day, something happened. No one knows for sure what it was, but an ailing Thomas sat wooden-faced, refusing to speak or to write. Somehow, he had come face to face with the Christ he studied.

"I cannot," he said. Pressed yet again, Thomas replied, "I can write no more. All that I have written seems like straw." And on that enigmatic note, the record of Thomas Aquina's life ends, the books never completed.

The wisdom of God is many-fold. That means God can write a

story of history, and in that story are deep spiritual implications for those involved. Further in, another layer deeper, is a reflection of our journey. Under that is yet another layer of spiritual realm reflection, and under that are types and shadows of Christ. Plunge still deeper, and there may be a foretelling of future, undergirded by a layer that would compel doctrine. Who can tell, what mind can contrive, what may yet be concealed beneath all of these? All from one simple historical account.

> **But as it is written, Eye hath not seen, nor ear heard, neither have entered into the heart of man, the things which God hath prepared for them that love him. (1 Corinthians 2:9)**

> **For whatsoever things were written aforetime were written for our learning, that we through patience and comfort of the scriptures might have hope. (Romans 15:4)**

This book contains several of these layers, partially exposed for your edification and revelation. I pray that the God of our Lord Jesus Christ would give unto you the Spirit of wisdom and revelation in truly knowing Christ in a deeper way. Through this history, I have woven in an imaginary story of a young man, Johanan. The name and lineage are Biblical, while the details are imaginary.

And to make plain [to everyone] the plan of the mystery [regarding the uniting of believing Jews and Gentiles into one

body] which [until now] was kept hidden through the ages in [the mind of] God who created all things. So now through the church the multifaceted wisdom of God [in all its countless aspects] might now be made known [revealing the mystery] to the [angelic] rulers and authorities in the heavenly places. This is in accordance with [the terms of] the eternal purpose which He carried out in Christ Jesus our Lord. (Ephesians 3:9-11 Amplified Bible)

I have extensively studied the timeline of the prophets and kings involved in this story. As much as possible, I have endeavored to keep the fictional story accurate to timelines laid out in Scriptures. However, not all scholars even agree on finer details of events, and the details I use are imaginary. I only ask that you look beyond the fictional story and possible disputes about timeline to consider the reality of spiritual significance I am trying to portray.

This story begs questions: where are you? In Babylon? On a trek? In a demolished Jerusalem? Have you built a temple in your life? Are the walls of your life repaired? Does the enemy fear you? Join me as we plunge beneath the surface.

Excursus

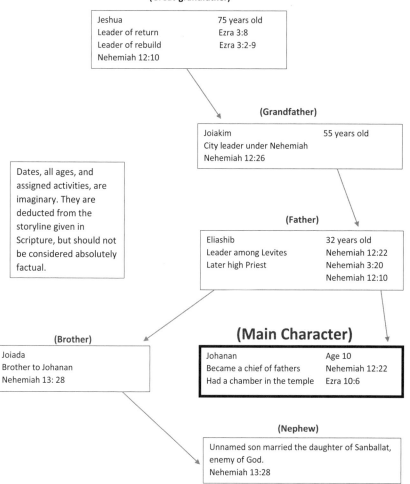

26   Much Rubbish

> **The rigors of endurance a journey requires can be furnished by a clear vision of intent and purpose.** -SS

CHAPTER 3

The Trek

The children of Judah were returning from a long period of exile. There were years of careless living followed by extreme suffering. They had been carried away in chains to a far country and forced to participate in a world and an economy that they hated.

During this period, the realization began to grow in them that the blatant disregard for God's law all around them was appalling. Desecration and idolatry were everywhere. There was no high praise, and most music and celebrations were centered around evil. Their servanthood and the constant humiliation and insults attacked their identity and drained their joy. Life was meaningless and empty.

When someone finally came to them with hope, they leapt to their feet in joy. Perhaps there was a chance! Inspired by this hope, they set out on the return trip ... home.

This trek was very difficult. It was hot, dusty, and dry. Bands of robbers watched greedily from the hills along the road. Towns along the way beckoned them to come in and stay. Perhaps some did stay, uninspired by the vision of the future. Maybe they simply became part of the landscape of those who hate God.

The cities along the path back to Jerusalem are full of them, these halfway folks ditching Babylon but not committed to Jerusalem. They while away their days in the parties and God-hating culture around them. The rebellion of their hearts becomes evident, and faced with the call to obedience, they dismiss it and dive into the next abomination, chortling about their freedom from Babylon. Their children grow up devastated, with no identity, with no ties to Jerusalem, and no inheritance there. If you are leaving Babylon, make sure you are totally committed to the obedience of Jerusalem. It is there you will find inheritance and blessing.

* * * *

Johanan sat on the knoll, arms around his knees, watching the sun slip over the horizon as the cactus owls began their all-night chorus. Johanan was deep in thought for a 10-year-old. Grandpa Joiakim had sat by the fire tonight with sage old Great-grandpa Jeshua. Grandpa could hardly remember Jerusalem, but Jeshua was full of stories about its busy markets, children at play in the streets, and its great feasts. He described solid rock walls with stones the size of an ox laid carefully in order. He told of the fortress-like towers that jutted up at intervals from the massive walls.

But most of all, Great-grandpa spoke reverently of the temple. Built with immaculate care, the temple had towered over the city. Huge, carved stone archways had sturdy cedar beam crossmembers. Gold sculptures gleamed everywhere in that temple. It was so beautiful, people came from the world over just to stand and admire its splendor. Towers on every corner outlined its glory.

Johanan's mind and imagination spun. His own father, Eliashib, had never seen Jerusalem. Grandpa was Johanan's age when he left. Repeatedly, Eliashib had asked for accounts of the ransacking of Jerusalem and the carrying away into captivity of its people. But Jeshua's mouth had always clamped shut, jaw muscles twitching. Sometimes he had sat as if in a trance, but he would not speak of those dark days.

Johanan's ten-year-old mind and imagination soared. He had been born in Babylon, and this pagan world was the only lifestyle he knew. His father, grandfather, and great-grandfather often sat and spoke in hushed tones of the city of Jerusalem. Great-grandpa especially would repeat long passages of what he called God's law. He told stories on the Sabbath too; not just stories of his boyhood past, but of long, long ago.

Johanan lay back against a rock and stared at the stars, remembering stories of Abraham and his God. He thought of the big flood, and of the ark a man named Noah had built at God's direction. His mind spun on to Joseph, the dreamer boy, and his years in prison. This, of course, led to the 400 years in Egypt and the slavery and abuse of the Israelites. Johanan grinned as he remembered his great-grandfather's rendition of the plague of stinking frogs.

According to Great-grandpa's accounts, God had brought plague after plague. Grandpa insisted their stories were all written on scrolls somewhere, but of course, Johanan had never seen them. The stories of how God had brought His people out of Egypt always tingled inside him, though. The crossing of the Red Sea and the giving of the Law to Moses were his favorites. He also liked the story of how Jericho fell.

But Johanan was riveted by the stories and legends of David. That a small shepherd boy could become the mightiest of warriors, and then KING! David's story and the Psalms the old folks chanted around the fires always sent warm rings around the heart of the young boy. He wasn't sure why . . . it just seemed that the whole scene meant that Johanan and his people were special to the Creator. Johanan heard his father's voice calling, and he jumped and hurried off to his bedroll.

*   *   *   *

Johanan jerked awake in the tent, and sat bolt upright. His eyes tried to adjust to the darkness around him. His father was giving orders in barely suppressed shouts, to his mother and siblings, as he buckled on his sword and knife, and dashed out into the night. His mother hurried over to him, to comfort him, but her own eyes betrayed real fear. "Shush now," she said comfortingly to Johanan.

In the distance there was shouting, screams of fright and pain, and fighting. Suddenly they were closer ... horses galloping right past the tent, footsteps, and shouted communication. The little family huddled together as the baby whimpered, and mom tried to comfort her.

The noise outside slowly subsided. Father returned, limping, tired, sweaty and nursing a gash on his left arm. Moms face went white when she saw it, and father held her while she choked back sobs. " Its Ok" he murmured. "Don't forget Whose we are."

Johanan lay pretending to sleep, while mom got warm water and salve around to clean up the wound. Father talked in quiet undertones to her as she worked. Johanan gathered that there were nearly 40 riders, a gang of local thieves. They had tried to make off with some of the cows, but then raided a tent also. The women screaming had set off the alarm through the camp. Father had rushed in and surprised a rider, who threw a spear at him, leaving a gash on his arm.

Several of the night herdsman, also mounted on horses, heard the ruckus and entered the fray. The robbers eventually fled, but two of them were killed in the conflict. The men in the caravan had animated discussions about these casualties, and whether they might make the future safer, or leave the caravan more subject to retributive attacks.

Johanan drifted off to sleep. He dreamed he was a grown man with a sword of his own, riding out of the broken-down gates of a city in the deep of night. He was following another man, a princely character with a steel resolve, and white hair. The older man in the lead, was adamant that the "walls must be built". "Get up", he insisted. "Get up......."

And there suddenly was his father in the morning light. "Get up, Johanan. It's time to get on with the trek."

Babylon just doesn't cut it. No matter how it is presented, Babel isn't what God's people were created for. Hearts yearn and cry. Spirits wilt, but continue to mourn softly. The song of Zion becomes a lonely wail, a hymn of past days. The songs speak of days of a presence, a connection, a power, and a joy, but the faces in the gathering disagree. History is elevated, and sermons and prayers of olden days are read and reread to wring the last drops of Shekinah glory from them.

Confusion comes in Babel. People speak past one another and cannot hear their brother. Women crawl into a shell. Youth reject the whole scene and simply identify as Babylonians. There is no Shekinah. The cloud and fire that guided Israel in the wilderness are distant memories, spoken of only by the old and a fringe group of radicals. It becomes reasonable to question why one would even serve this God.

Then a return begins. Some are excited, some are angry, and some are hurt. It is difficult to understand when all one has ever known is Babylon. It is even more formidable to try to explain to neighbors that the God of Jerusalem is calling you to leave what is real and present simply to pursue a dream. Leaving the tried and proven for the unknown is always difficult. It is always a risk, and some of your closest friends will stay in Babylon.

Don't be too hard on those who dwell in the land and have become accustomed to it. Ask for their support and blessing, and then head for Jerusalem. It wasn't easy for Abraham either.

Remember when leaving not to take the idolatry of towers with you. Jerusalem has no room for Babel. Worship has no agreement with the drive to somehow be better than others. The tribalism, the superiority, and the agreements with heathen culture—these all stay behind in Babylon where they belong.

Take the gold with you, however; gold represents Divine Nature. All that you have found that is of God or represents the divine will be needed where you are going. Ask those who stay in Babylon if they have extra for you.

I find it a travesty that the people of God today have more in common with Babylon than with Jerusalem.

And whosoever remaineth in any place where he sojourneth, let the men of his place help him with silver, and with gold, and with goods, and with beasts, beside the freewill offering for the house of God that is in Jerusalem. (Ezra 1:4)

The theme of Babylon and how it holds the people of God captive runs all through Scripture. In Revelation 18:4, Babylon still shows up, having become a center for all devils and foul spirits. Once again, a voice comes from heaven, both commanding and pleading, "Come out of her, my people, lest you take part in her sins."

I find it a travesty that the people of God today have more in common with Babylon than with Jerusalem. The concept of a separated people, called by His name, with an allegiance to another country and city, is all but gone. More effort is employed in trying to hide our identity in the marketplace than in displaying it.

Where is Daniel?

Where is Jeshua?

Where is Zerubbabel?

Ezekiel saw a vision around the time of Nebuchadnezzar of an angel who was sent with ink to mark those who wept and sighed over the sins of Jerusalem and her people. Would you be marked by that angel? (Ezekiel 9:4)

And the Lord said unto him, Go through the midst of the city, through the midst of Jerusalem, and set a mark upon the foreheads of the men that sigh and that cry for all the abominations that be done in the midst thereof. Ezekiel 9:4

It is a long road back from Babylon to Jerusalem. No man should start to build a tower unless he has enough resources to finish it. If you want to stop living in confusion and come into the mount of worship, be alerted that the journey back is more brutal and fraught with peril than you have imagined. But systems of men, built with bricks of human desire and straw of human effort, will never satisfy the deep cry within. Jerusalem calls and promises fulfillment of spirit, for it is your native home, and the only place your spirit will ever find rest. Are you ready for the trek?

Q. What do you see as the Babylonish systems around you in your area and culture?

_____
_____
_____
_____
_____

Q. Would you say that you have been captive to them? Why or why not?

_____
_____
_____
_____
_____

Q. What does a journey "back" look like to you? Do you have the strength to make it?

_____
_____
_____
_____
_____

> That to which you ascribe meaning, becomes the controlling value of your life. These values and principles demand a foundation outside of themselves; otherwise, they are simply a chosen illusion. -SS

CHAPTER 4

Foundations

Johanan was literally trembling with excitement. Today was the day... the long-awaited day. Weeks of trudging across desert were over, and today they would round the last curve in the valley and see Jerusalem. Images floated in his mind. He looked down at his hands and laughed as he saw them shaking. His father, Eliashib, also seemed excited. A new light had gleamed in his eyes ever since they had crossed the Jordan River.

Grandpa was also acting a bit strange, Johanan noticed. But it was Great-grandpa Jeshua who had gone completely silent. Even the donkey he rode seemed to have its head down. They rounded the last curve and crested a small hill.

And there it was—Jerusalem! Excitement ran high as they approached the city. Shouting, running, weeping, and general chaos erupted. Long-lost cousins who had never met embraced and clung to one another as inhabitants of Jerusalem came to meet the newcomers. The travelers started fires, began to cook, and set up their tents.

Amid the hubbub, Johanan sat on a broken rock, surveying the scene. Only one wall remained of the once-glorious temple. Streets were filled with debris. Burned-out houses lay in ruins, and the walls of the city had gaping holes. As he watched, a fox trotted out from under a pile of stones, climbed over the wall, and disappeared.

Johanan tried to identify what he felt so deep inside. Was it disappointment? This ruined city was nothing like Great-grandpa had described. Was it sadness he felt? Depression? Hopelessness? Fear? His father was busily talking with relatives, drowning his own emotion in words. Grandpa was off with other leaders, looking at possible next steps.

Maybe Great-grandpa would explain it all. Johanan saw him standing on a broken wall by the temple and ran to him.

"Father Jeshua," he began. There was no response. Strange. He tugged on the old man's robe.

"Father . . ." but something stopped him. He looked up. A strange, deep, moaning, soul-piercing wail of grief escaped Great-grandpa. Sobbing, he slumped to the ground, wailing aloud. Johanan stood riveted in shock. Then slowly, that same grief of deep loss rose up in him too. He crumpled to his knees beside Jeshua, and together they wept in a deep groaning of agony over a loss they had no words for.

Days passed. The men gathered in groups, discussing points of action. They began to segregate into smaller groups by city and by area. One by one, these groups departed to the location of their family inheritance. Back to Bethlehem, back to Hebron, back to Jericho. Johanan was sad to see so many friends leave, but he soon forgot it amid all the work.

Great-grandpa Jeshua pointed the family to the houses that were family possession. They began the backbreaking work of moving the debris out, removing loose stones, and digging down to solid foundations. Only then did they mix mortar, fetch stones, and rebuild the walls. Many of the stones weighed more than Johanan did, and he watched in awe as Grandpa and Dad rigged scaffolding, ramps, crane-jigs, and movers to install the stones. That was followed by installing the roof timbers. Throughout the process, Jeshua mostly just gave direction to the work because of his age.

Seven months passed. Houses were well underway, and some were already livable. The market had opened, and locals from the countryside sold produce, pottery, meat, and cheese. The streets were slowly being cleared.

Early one morning, a trumpet sounded. Over the next several days, people appeared from every direction, traveling in small groups. Great-grandpa Jeshua had been busy for days, but Johanan didn't understand what was happening. Many evenings, his father and grandpa would spend hours poring over some ancient scroll. Sometimes they read aloud from it, and Johanan like that. The words felt so clean, as if they would wash you like water.

The people gathered at the site of the ruined temple. In the courtyard, they erected once again the altar of God. Johanan fairly swelled as he saw Great-grandpa Jeshua giving the orders. Just before sundown, Grandpa appeared, leading a young bullock. Johana stood with his mother and watched as his father, Eliashib, slit the animal's throat in front of 100,000 people. Several uncles gathered around and lifted the animal onto the wood. The fire crackled, and the burnt offering was made. Some people wept softly. Others stood with hands raised. Off to one side, a group of singers chanted Psalms.

Something happened that day. Deep in the evening, Johanan began to comprehend a deeper level of the return to Jerusalem. A reality of his God, a reality of His presence, the purity of His law, the absoluteness of His justice, the meaning of life ... it all began to make sense. From that day on, Johanan's life was changed.

Every morning and evening, a sacrifice was offered on that altar. Many times, his dad was involved.

"It's because we are Levites," he explained to Johanan. "Long ago, God called the tribe of Levi to be His priests and to serve in His temple."

The people also held large feasts with many offerings. They came from all over the nation, bringing gifts. Great-grandpa Jeshua had constructed a special storehouse for all the gifts, the food, and the donations.

Now in the second year of their coming unto the house of God at Jerusalem, in the second month, began Zerubbabel the son of Shealtiel, and Jeshua the son of Jozadak, and the remnant of their brethren the priests and the Levites, and all they that were come out of the captivity unto Jerusalem; and appointed the Levites, from twenty years old and upward, to set forward the work of the house of the Lord. (Ezra 3:8)

People like Jeshua never lost sight of the rebuilding of the temple.

It is a long distance from Babylon to Jerusalem. It's a long journey from a human system to a true place of worship that God accepts. Building an altar in Babylon won't work. Even in Jerusalem, where a temple SHOULD be, building an altar is good. But the altar and the sacrifice, along with all the gifts, still don't equal a temple.

The journey back was completed. The returnees were doing extensive repair to their inheritances all over the nation. They were reading the Law of Moses again, they had built the altar, they were keeping feasts, and even celebrating entire days of rejoicing and praise.

Still, there was no temple. Faithful people with a vision donated money for the purpose. Leaders hired the best available draftsmen and architects to begin designing a temple. They spent long hours studying, discussing, reading, and drafting. Treasurers counted the gifts and payments that had been offered and sent them to Zidon and Tyre of Lebanon to purchase cedar beams. They cleared the temple area of rubble. Priests were outfitted with priestly garments and trained in what their duties were toward God and the people.

Zerubbabel worked tirelessly, moving among priests, building location, messengers, and the stone quarry. Jeshua helped some, gave on-site direction, and worked at educating all the men involved in the work. At this point, one thing consumed the focus of all those working in Jerusalem: *the foundation.*

> ***It is the wisdom of the ancients, to seek the most solid of foundations, upon which to build that which is eternal.***

The foundation is the grounding point, the resting place, and the anchor of the building. And this was not just any building. It was the temple. Everything it rested on had to be bedrock or else founded on bedrock. It had to be immovable. If it moved even a little, the entire temple would be at risk! Some of the stones in the foundation weighed around 600 TONS. This was not some muscle-jacked rock masons mudding 80-pound stones into place. This was foundation.

Building a temple is hard work. It all begins with foundation. Somehow, there needs to be an established bedrock of realities that cannot be moved. Even before that, there must be a daily altar of sacrifice, a place where we come to meet with and cry out to the living God of eternity and creation. Then the work of foundations can commence.

Babylon (system of men) did not destroy the temple because the foundations were bad. Rather, the temple was leveled and the city burned because of disobedience. If the TRUE HABITATION of God has been disrupted in your life and needs to be rebuilt, start with the daily sacrifice of praise. Then begin to dig through the rubble of the past teachings, doctrine, practice, and ordinances. All the while, seek FOUNDATIONS.

If the foundations be destroyed, what can the righteous do? Psalm 11:3

There are solid, foundational realities that the temple rests upon. God is right, and His ways are right. He created the earth with intention. Jesus Christ, the Son of God, the Lamb of God, came to earth to shed His perfect blood for the redemption of man. He is calling you. Believe Him.

But without faith it is impossible to please him: for he that cometh to God must believe that he is, and that he is a rewarder of them that diligently seek him. (Hebrews 11:6)

I could go on and on about foundation stones. It is not, however, my purpose here to lay all the foundation stones for a temple in your life. Rather, YOU must discover and recognize the foundation. This is all simply to point you toward the basic, elementary, foundational stones that must be in place before a temple can be built. Ultimately, all of it must come into alignment with the Chief Cornerstone, Jesus Christ. (1 Peter 2:6)

For other foundation can no man lay than that is laid, which is Jesus Christ. (1 Corinthians 3:11)

And are built upon the foundation of the apostles and prophets, Jesus Christ himself being the chief corner stone. (Ephesians 2:20)

Wherefore also it is contained in the scripture, Behold, I lay in Sion a chief corner stone, elect, precious: and he that believeth on him shall not be confounded. (1 Peter 2:6)

We live in an era of extreme selfishness. The ways of God, the truth of His Word, the power of His Christ, and His claim on our obedience have all come into question. Fat and full of pleasures, we have doggedly persisted in our disobedience. While we slept, the world systems have come in and taken us captive. Too drunk with our own superiority to notice, we slogged off in chains to Babylon, where we built large towers to reach heaven. Incidentally, going forward is not the answer. Going back is.

"New" ideas about Scripture that try to align the Bible with Babylon are foolishness. They are, in fact, a reflection of why the captivity of Babylon exists. This is not a time for more buildings, bigger stages, more lights, louder sounds, or better smoke and mirrors. Neither is it a time for more rules, stricter governance, control, and superiority of righteousness. We don't need better sermons and more polished speakers. A pile of manmade bricks of human desire and human effort to polish up human behavior will build a tower of Babel, but it will never work for a temple.

Foundations must be uncovered. They are there, covered by piles of manmade rubble. Finding and repairing them will be hard, but it must be done. Seek out the eternal, immovable aspects of faith without regard for Babylon's input or viewpoint.

> *If you are in Babylon, going forward isn't the answer. Going back is the answer.*

Turning toward Jerusalem is easy. Finding the new birth is relatively painless. Building a time and place of worship—your altar—takes a little effort. But uncovering and repairing foundations? Preparing your life to be a temple of the holy glory of God? Building a place of communion that communicates the love of an eternal God for all nations?

That's a whole different level.

> But many of the priests and Levites and chief of the fathers, who were ancient men, that had seen the first house, when the foundation of this house was laid before their eyes, wept with a loud voice; and many shouted aloud for joy: So that the people could not discern the noise of the shout of joy from the noise of the weeping of the people: for the people shouted with a loud shout, and the noise was heard afar off. (Ezra 3:12-13)

Johanan watched in awe as the priests, all in full dress and in order, raised their trumpets. The Levites started the music with a clanging of cymbals. The trumpets chimed in, followed by thousands of voices, praising the Lord because His mercy endureth forever.

The foundation was laid. People cheered ecstatically. Euphoria filled the air as the noise continued to build to a dramatic crescendo.

Johanan yelled, hands over his ears, into the electric atmosphere. Then he saw Jeshua. Somehow, he looked old. Johanan moved toward the front of the crowd, closer to Great-grandpa. Then he heard it. The same wail, the heartbroken, wounded sense of loss rising in a sobbing cry from Jeshua. Still, the noise around grew louder. Some were wailing, and others were praising in ecstatic joy. Tens of thousands of voices shouting together could be heard afar off. Because real, rock-solid foundations existed once again.

Q. What do you see as foundations in your own life?

_____
_____
_____
_____
_____

Q. What do you see as foundations in your church?

_____
_____
_____
_____
_____

Q. What do you think was the emotion old man Jeshua had as he wailed? Have you ever felt that kind of emotion for the Church and its condition today?

_____
_____
_____
_____
_____

Much Rubbish

> Very little of value is ever accomplished without resistance. The realm of darkness always tries to choke light. -SS

CHAPTER 5

Resistance

Whenever the people of God abandon the holds of Babel and begin again to worship, sacrifice, and praise, enemies will appear.
Now when the adversaries of Judah and Benjamin heard that the children of the captivity builded the temple unto the Lord God of Israel; Then they came to Zerubbabel, and to the chief of the fathers, and said unto them, Let us build with you: for we seek your God, as ye do; and we do sacrifice unto him since the days of Esarhaddon king of Assur, which brought us up hither. (Ezra 4:1-2)
If you have laid the foundations in your life, the enemies of God around you will smell a rat very quickly. Generally, the first order of attack is a friendly offer to help. In the story we are examining, the enemies in the land represent devils and unclean spirits. It should not come as a surprise, therefore, that having them involved in temple building may not be the best idea.
We noted earlier that Babylon is often mentioned in Scripture, some 294 times. It carries a type with it. So do the enemies of

the Lord. It will be impossible to effectively deal with these enemies unless we gain some consciousness of the spirit world and the realities there. Scripture does not record how they were determined by the leaders, Zerubbabel and Jeshua, to be enemies. It simply states that they were, in fact, adversaries.

David was one of the mightiest warriors Israel ever knew. He surrounded himself with three mighty men, and around them, a rank of thirty mighty men. The three mightiest would go into a formation and fight their way directly through an enemy battalion. Yet, in David's last words, he declared that the real enemies of God cannot be taken with hands.

But the sons of Belial shall be all of them as thorns thrust away, because they cannot be taken with hands. (2 Samuel 23:6)

Jesus cast out devils wherever He went during His years of ministry. There was direct conflict between the Temple that He was and the realm of darkness. Regardless of how temptation or trickery was presented to Him, He never even came close to taking the bait. Satan asked for only a teeny-weeny secret agreement in exchange for giving Jesus a kingdom.

Again, the devil taketh him up into an exceeding high mountain, and sheweth him all the kingdoms of the world, and the glory of them; And saith unto him, All these things will I give thee, if thou wilt fall down and worship me. Then saith Jesus unto him, Get thee hence, Satan: for it is written, Thou shalt worship the Lord thy God, and him only shalt thou serve. (Matthew 4:8-10)

There is absolutely nothing to gain by making agreements with the adversaries of God.

Jesus, with His eye on the cross, said no. There is absolutely nothing to gain by making agreements with the adversaries of God. As we shall see later on, every agreement ends up costing far too much. Paul also refers to the enemies we must face, calling them gods, principalities, spiritual wickedness, and demonic (unclean: Greek *akarthos,* demonic). The injunction is always to separate from all of them, so God can be our Father.

Wherefore come out from among them, and be ye separate, saith the Lord, and touch not the unclean thing; and I will receive you. And will be a Father unto you, and ye shall be my sons and daughters, saith the Lord Almighty. (2 Corinthians 6: 17, 18)

If you do not allow the local demons of fear, shame, etc. to help build your temple, they will begin to weaken your hands. They will also begin to seek information on where your weak spots are so they can trouble you. After that, they will seek to influence authorities against you.

Then the people of the land weakened the hands of the people of Judah, and troubled them in building, And hired counsellors against them, to frustrate their purpose, all the days of Cyrus king of Persia, even until the reign of Darius king of Persia. (Ezra 4:4-5)

The adversaries seem to understand something that often escapes those who seek to build a temple. They know that the day the temple is completed, a strange power will descend. That power will rule and dominate all enemies around that place. In this case, the adversaries reported to the king that this city and temple were seditious.

They were right about that, you know. This city doesn't deal well with submission to other nations with other gods. And yes, if the temple is built and the walls repaired, and if the God of the city comes down to dwell there, the city will become an entity of dominion.

*　　*　　*　　*

Johanan paused his chiseling and wiped his brow. At 15 years old, he was expected to do the work of a man, and he had been assigned to remove old mortar from stones designated for use in rebuilding. It was hard work, and sometimes it took the efforts of three men to turn a stone over. A movement caught Johanan's attention, and he turned to see a procession of men, soldiers, and horses coming up the valley.

He felt momentary fear, but then walked over to his father and alerted him. The workers and overseers gathered together. Bisham, Mithredath, Tabeel . . . Johanan heard the names. The group had come from farther north with their servants to help with the building of the temple of God.

Johanan saw Great-grandpa's shoulders stiffen. The old man shuffled forward, his age showing, but courage, determination, and fierceness still emanating from him.

"No!" declared Great-grandpa to the intruders. "You have nothing to do with us to build a house to our God."

Just like that, the meeting was over. Johanan wondered at the terseness of Jeshua's approach. Still, Jeshua had been around a long time, and he probably knew a few things.

Over the next several years, as the project moved slowly along, Johanan saw more meetings, more arguments, and more frustrations from this crowd. Slowly, he began to understand that these men, pleasant and gracious as they appeared, carried a very deep and sinister desire to stop the temple of God. They wrote letters to Babylon, to Shushan, and to Persepolis, where Artaxerxes had his palace.

Some kings seem to have been favorable to the temple, while some were not. King Ahasuerus, for example, seems to have gotten his letter soon after he married Esther and hanged Haaman. It is difficult to establish a clear timeline during this period. Scholars vary in their dates and estimates by up to 75 years. Part of the reason is the kings mentioned. There were kings in Babylon and in Shushan, 300 miles to the east, and in Persepolis (Iran) some 700 miles from Babylon. The stories of Daniel took place in Babylon, while the setting for Mordecai and Esther's story was in Shushan. Artaxerxes was in Persepolis. Some scholars estimate the temple was halted for three years, while others believe it could have been as long as seventeen years. But most agree that it was halted for a period.

* * * *

Johanan sat by the fire, admiring the beautiful woman who was stirring the flames with a stick. He could hardly believe he and Havilah were actually married. It seemed like only days ago that he and his father Eliashib had made the heart-stopping trek to her father's house to ask for her hand. Then there was the wedding, and a feast of celebration, and a blessing from the community...

His reverie interrupted by a sudden commotion, Johanan grabbed a torch, and he and Havilah moved toward the small community group near the temple. He looked around the faces and saw Dad, Grandpa, numerous uncles, cousins, and even Great-grandpa and Zerubbabel.

A man was speaking, his voice raised. The words were firm, clear, and seemed to pierce like a sword. Johanan stood in shock. He knew and admired Haggai, but he had never seen him like this. His voice was raised, but not angry. Zachariah his friend stood off to the side, watching and nodding. The words cut to the heart.

In the second year of Darius the king, in the sixth month, in the first day of the month, came the word of the Lord by Haggai the prophet unto Zerubbabel the son of Shealtiel, governor of Judah, and to Joshua the son of Josedech, the high priest, saying, Thus speaketh the Lord of hosts, saying, This people say, The time is not come, the time that the Lord's house should be built. Then came the word of the Lord by Haggai the prophet, saying, Is it time for you, O ye, to dwell in your cieled houses, and this house lie waste? Now therefore thus saith the Lord of hosts; Consider your ways. Ye have sown much, and bring in little; ye eat, but ye have not enough; ye drink, but ye are not filled with drink; ye clothe you, but there is none warm; and he that earneth wages earneth wages to put it into a bag with holes. Thus saith the Lord of hosts; Consider your ways. Go up to the mountain, and bring wood, and build the house; and I will take pleasure in it, and I will be glorified, saith the Lord. (Haggai 1:1-8)

The words stopped flowing. Zerubbabel and Jeshua stood with their heads down. Then, as if on cue, the two men looked up and locked eyes. Pure power flowed from them as they turned to address the group.

"He is right," they declared. "It is the word of the Lord."

Conversations exploded on all sides. God had just spoken clearly through a prophet! Haggai was gone, having disappeared into the shadows, but when Jeshua announced that building would resume the next day, a great cheer went up.

On the word of the Lord, people went to work again. All the harassment and even letters from the king were as a distant memory. As they worked, Johanan thought about the visions he had as a boy while traveling across the desert. He smiled, but the enemies did not. Enraged, they sent a letter to King Darius by Priority Pony Express.

The king did his own research and wrote a scathing letter in reply. Stop hindering the work, it said, and immediately give the builders any supplies they need.

The God of heaven wants His temple built. He wants it built in you, and He wants you built into His temple. The King of heaven will move whoever and whatever He needs to if you are ready to listen to the prophets. Anyone who stands in the way of this temple risks making their own house a dunghill.

> **Also I have made a decree, that whosoever shall alter this word, let timber be pulled down from his house, and being set up, let him be hanged thereon; and let his house be made a dunghill for this. (Ezra 6:11)**

It is not God's desire for His people to live in a land of plenty and disregard Him as God. A time of peace and plenty is an invitation to revel in His goodness and shout praises while showing His glory to all men. However, times of ease tend to make folks unthankful. This selfish attitude makes people careless about obedience. Unthankful disobedience lands us in the nightmare of bondage in Babylon, but God's desire is not for His people to live there. He places in their hearts a cry and longing for real worship in a real temple in Jerusalem.

God does not only seek hatred for Babylon within His people. Rather, He wants them to be driven by a true desire to know Him, to worship at His feet, and to experience the cloud and fire of His presence. People are motivated to leave Babylon, and many do leave. Strong desire is required just for this step alone. While trapped by Babylonian kings of fear, control, religion, witchcraft, hatred, and addictions, only the Spirit of truth can produce enough hope or desire to escape. The trip back home is harsh and painful. It is not God's desire for His people to only make the trip back, nor to live on the ruins of what once was. The past, regardless of its grandeur, will not sustain the future. Intrinsic value is attached to the future. This is why desire is a tree of life, and hope makes not ashamed.

God does not want His people to content themselves with the normal pursuits of life while the temple lies abandoned. Apostle Paul tells the Corinthians, **"Ye are the temple of the living God." (2 Corinthians 6:16)**

It is not God's desire that His people live in their inheritance and build the temple while still having their lives exposed to the enemy. He wants a wall and gates for protection. He desires to establish His glory among the people in a magnificent city. (Revelation 21:10-12)

And the enemies of God will always squawk and protest about each step.

They will try to keep you in Babylon.

They will harass you during your return trip.

They will threaten you.

They will mock you.

They will deceitfully try to "help" you.

They will seek to get you stopped.

They will distract you.

They will try to kill you.

They will try to enslave you.

They will even purchase rooms in your temple.

Don't buy it ... any of it. His lies and resistance are futile. Look in the back of the Book for the ending. We win. Press on in clarity and truth, and build to please God.

Q. If you look at Jerusalem as your life, personally, what enemies do you see as forces that hate the idea of your building a temple?

_____

_____

_____

_____

_____

Q. Do you see enemies of God trying to help build the church? What enemies?

_____

_____

_____

_____

_____

Q. What do you think people normally do when facing resistance to the building of a temple in their lives?

_____

_____

_____

_____

_____

Much Rubbish

> **It is a simple truth, that when man wants to connect with God, he needs to go to the Temple. The Temple is the established dwelling of God, and a place of worship. -SS**

CHAPTER 6

Temple

While his great-grandpa Jeshua performed the evening sacrifices, Johanan knelt reverently on the stone atrium. His mind went back over the last 15 years, and he recalled the long, hot, grueling journey from Babylon. The day they rounded the last curve and he saw for the first time the ruins of the once proud city of Jerusalem was etched in his memory. Johanan's eyes moistened as he recalled the tears and wailing of Jeshua that first night. He relived the deep emotion, the longing, the cry of his own heart. His face softened, and he raised his hands in worship and praise to the God of his fathers.

As he praised God, Johanan's mind wondered to his wife, Havilah. Even her name was musical and sweet. She had brought so much depth, beauty, and meaning to his life. His hands still raised, Johanan's mind continued to the two sons and darling daughters God had graciously sent to them.

At the altar, Jeshua chanted prayer as the offering burned. The words of the singers off to the side floated on the breeze. Johanan opened his eyes and looked at the scene. The foundation of the temple had been laid years before. King Artaxerxes had halted the building process for a while (Ezra 4:23-24) and not much had been done for a long time. During that period, Johanan had finished his own house and was quite happy with the results.

After a push from the prophets, the rebuilding of the temple resumed. More letters were sent, to both King Artaxerxes in Persepolis and his brother Darius in Babylon. But this time, both responded with a very positive message to the Jewish people: BUILD the temple. (Ezra 6:11-12, and 7:11)

The scene in front of Johanan now was of that ongoing build. Timbers were lying off to one side. Huge stones were cut for upper arches. The crane apparatus towered above it all, and the scene was a tribute to excellency of both engineering and architecture. The smoke of the sacrifice rose through the frameworks as Grandpa Joiakim helped with procedures. The Psalms off to the side brought a deep settled peace, and once again Johanan realized why.

Why the journey...
Why the people...
Why the city...
Why the building...
Why the sacrifice...
Why the temple... the temple of the living God. It was to be a place for His glory, for Him to dwell among His people, and for them to experience His Presence. That feeling of longing, of commitment, of strength of purpose, washed over Johanan again. As he walked home, he considered once more how to build.

Nebuchadnezzar had come from Babylon and destroyed the temple some 55 years before. The people were enslaved, killed, or driven out of the area. For 40 years, there had been no sacrifice, no feasts, no celebrations, no song. Forty years of no connection, no cloud or pillar of fire, and no experience of connecting to the glory of God.

Of course, this drought of connection to God came AFTER people had rejected Him for decades and disobeyed Him for a long time. Perhaps some hardly even noticed the loss of connection. Others, however, wept at the loss. Jeremiah saw it coming, and he wept until he felt his eyes were rivers. Daniel carried his faith in the living God right into Babylon with purpose of heart. And as they built the second temple, some old men could still remember the glory of the first temple built by Solomon. But the ark of the covenant from the first temple was lost, never to be seen again.

* * * *

The first issue to consider in leaving Babylon and returning to Jerusalem is the temple. Babylon vandalized and stole from the temple. Then they threw it down and took the gold from it. Gold in Scripture represents the divine. In the Middle-eastern mindset of the Old Testament period, the outcome of a war had less to do with the size and strength of the armies than with the God (or god) they worshiped.

When the Babylonians came against Judah, the people were afraid, but they clung to hope in their God. When that same God sent a message through Jeremiah saying they would be overthrown for their sins, they threw him into a pit.

The population was devastated, therefore, when the god of Babylon came out looking like the winner. The people of Judah thought they possessed the divine because they had the temple, but it was destroyed and the gold stolen. In the aftermath, a few people like Daniel never lost track of their God. Daniel prayed three times a day with his window open toward Jerusalem, and he did so even at the risk of his own life.

There will always be those few who pledge their allegiance to a God Who seems to have lost, even under duress in Babylon. As the song says, "Honor them the faithful few, all hail to Daniel's band." But for all who return to Jerusalem, the habitation of God and the place of real relationship, the temple is a must. The temple in your life represents a place of living connection with God. This is where God dwells, from whence His voice speaks. It is a place for the divine within you. It is a place of sacrifice and blood, as well as of continual praise, adoration, and worship. The fire and cloud come and abide there.

This is true both individually and corporately. The return of the Jews stirred up some intense emotion in the enemies around them. The building of the temple evoked even more. They sought to hinder the work, to restrict funding, and to stop progress. Your enemies, the demons and unclean spirits around you, become agitated when you start restoring a real relationship with Christ. They will fuss and fume and send letters of accusation to the "king" to halt your progress. They may even succeed for a while.

Persevere anyway.

There IS a presence of the living God available both to individuals and to groups. There is a glory—divine glory—for you to walk and worship in. There is an altar of truth on which to offer sacrifices of praise and adoration. There is a place you can live where continuous praise wells up out of your inner being and sustains you through the hardest times.

Most of us are familiar with the concept of being born again. To many of us, that seems like a once-and-done event, a point of collision with an eternal, holy God where we are completely changed. We expect everything to be different after that, and it is.

However, it takes time for us to recognize and experience what has transpired in fact. When the Jews returned to Jerusalem, they rebuilt the temple. They started by establishing the foundation. This foundation brought an extreme outburst of emotion. The people wept and shouted, and the commotion was heard far away. (Ezra 3:12-13)

The event also began a stirring among the enemies around them. The new birth is not an end in our life; rather, it is a beginning. This birth is the foundation of a temple God wants to build in us and with us. This temple will be filled with praises and with the presence of God.

The foundation of this temple in our life is the new birth. This occurs when the Word of God enters us, we receive it (Him), and the Spirit of Christ comes into us to set up His throne in our spirit.

But ye are not in the flesh, but in the Spirit, if so be that the Spirit of God dwell in you. Now if any man have not the Spirit of Christ, he is none of his. (Romans 8:9)

Being born again, not of corruptible seed, but of incorruptible, by the word of God, which liveth and abideth for ever. (1 Peter 1:23)

The entrance of His Spirit often brings both weeping and shouting. Filled with the emotions and praise, it is easy to believe the temple is already complete. But this is only the beginning.

My little children, of whom I travail in birth again until CHRIST be formed in you. (Galatians 4:19)

The building of the temple in Jerusalem took much personal sacrifice over many years. Coming out of Babylon is tough. The trek can be exhausting. Building the temple takes time and energy. It also attracts the attention of the enemies around Jerusalem . . . the evil and unclean spirits. At this point, however, they are not so afraid. In fact, they will offer to help build your temple if you will let them. (Ezra 4:1-3)

By the way, having your enemies help you build a temple is a really good example of a really bad idea. Renting a room in the temple of God to an enemy is an even worse idea. (Nehemiah

13:7-8) Lay the foundation carefully. Establish a legacy of praise immediately. Build with commitment. Don't make friends with the Lord's enemies.

And don't go back to Babylon.

Praise runs all the way through the scene of the temple. David had established this habit many years before in the Psalms. Then he prophesied that YOU, another generation to come, would praise Him. (Psalm 102:18) The praise of the Lord ringing loudly in the temple as it is built is not just a pleasant idea. It must happen.

In today's world, we have come to expect the instant, microwaveable, just-add-water, pre-packaged copies of the real thing. By contrast, God is not interested in a cheap imitation. He insists on the genuine, and it takes years to develop to a place of solid maturity. More than 13 years were spent building the temple in Ezra's day. Being born again may well happen in an instant, but maturing in our walk with God, learning to hear Him, and allowing Him to speak into our nature until we are clean and our motives are purified will take time.

The principle of building a Temple is simple: Hear, Do.

Allow Him to do this in you. Build on the foundation of a Christ-centered new birth and a conscious, continued acknowledgment of His presence. Hear and do. Seek revelation, and act on it. (Matthew 7:24) All the while, let there be rejoicing and praise! Returning from Babylon is no small thing. Let that reality sustain you when things seem otherwise dried up and difficult. A spirit of worship in the temple has a way of striking fear into the enemies of God while it builds in us a habitation of glory. (2 Corinthians 3:18)

Many of God's people today once again lie in the bondage of Babylon. Too many constituents of the way of God lie trampled under the altars of education and intellectualism. The temple of God is ignored or relegated to a distant second priority, and it soon lies covered in the dust of the forgotten. Slowly, the kings of culture encroach on the land, surrounding the city of God. Even though some groups labor hard at building the walls, even though a few Jeremiahs weep and pound pulpits, and even though God Himself warns, there is no repentance. True repentance and a crying out to KNOW the eternal God is often viewed as extreme, unnecessary, or even foolish.

Then the Nebuchadnezzars of pride, selfishness, rejection, uncleanness, defilement, and isolationism break down the walls of the city and haul God's people off to Babylon. Alone, rejected, defiled, and hopeless, they sit by the river in Babylon. They cannot sing, and they hang their harps on the willows. (Psalm 137)

Struggling to maintain an identity as people who belong to God, they press on as servants to a foreign king. Regardless of what is produced, most of it has to be given to their captors. The reality they find in the Word of God is paid out in tribute to those who are no gods. Or people simply acquiesce and give of their time, talents, abilities, and bodies directly to the enterprise of Babylon itself.

Think about it. How much time is given to Babylon? How much of life consists of pursuits and endeavors in alignment with enemies of the God of eternity? How much of life is actually babble, instead of LIFE?

We have noted earlier that Babylon is portrayed in Scripture as that which corrupts and confuses. God presents His Spirit as altogether different:

For God hath not given us the spirit of fear; but of power, and of love, and of a sound mind. (2 Timothy 1:7)

In the New Testament, this concept of Babylon is often depicted as "the world." People and churches wake up one day to find themselves enslaved to something they cannot see and have no idea how to oppose. Homes lie in shambles. Relationships are cold and distant. The youth are more interested in games and parties than in knowing God. Friends lie wallowing in addiction. Depression has become a plague. Children are abused by parents and wives by husbands. Sexual abuse torments minds and hearts, shattering hope of the future and wrecking marriages. Men know more about the god of the NFL than the God of Israel. People sleep through a sermon, but shout and scream about a game as if it mattered. Thousands of hours are plowed into contracts with the god of mammon. Woman bow down to gods of fashion, worshipping before a mirror, painting, puffing, and fluffing.

The spirits behind these gods torment and create even more havoc in lives. Families separate. Infidelity explodes. Divorce becomes normal. Children hurt. Addictions blossom. Churches split. Rage, murder, and abortion occur. Youth reject the whole scene.

Others take a different approach; they simply pay Babylon off. Blind to the fact that they are servants to a Babylonish system, they thicken and heighten walls. Yet every day, most of what they grow or produce is paid to the world system. Sermons, meetings, attention, and thought is paid out in focus to the dreaded WORLD.

Certain that they are doing right, they are horrified to find Babylon creeping into their own house. But they awaken one day to find rejection, anger, bitterness, witchcraft, and lust napping on their couch. Relationships fail. People cut themselves. Anger and sexual abuse have their way.

On Sundays, God's people gather. They commemorate a time when the presence of God was among His people and in His temple. They speak of hope in a time when it may be like that once more.

But the resources of the people are expended in divorce support groups, AA meetings, yoga, abortion rehab, drug programs, politics, and seminars about sexual abuse, domestic violence, and forgiveness. They build huge buildings, educate pastors, write books, and found treatment centers for sexual addictions.

But where is the temple? Where is the pillar and cloud of His manifest presence? God wants a return. His heart cries for a people who will return to build a temple for His name. He wants those who will carry His glory to the nations. Can you hear His Spirit calling for that return and that temple?

For ye are the temple of the living God; as God hath said, I will dwell in them, and walk in them; and I will be their God, and they shall be my people. (2 Corinthians 6:16b)

There will indeed be a return. Some of you are already on the long, hot journey back to Jerusalem from Babylon. Some of you soon will be. Some were born in Babylon and expect nothing better. For those with the courage to return, it will be a rough journey back. The devastation left behind is staggering.

There is much rubbish.

But God will have a people, and they shall be His temple. (1 Corinthians 3:16) The foundation is the apostles and prophets, and Jesus Christ Himself is the Chief Cornerstone. Each one of us is going to build the temple in our own life, and then we will be built into a beautiful, glorious habitation of God together. This will take years of hard work. It will require careful attention to blueprint and to detail.

In whom all the building fitly framed together groweth unto an holy temple in the Lord: In whom ye also are builded together for an habitation of God through the Spirit. (Ephesians 2:21, 22)

In the end, the presence and power of God will once again be with His people. Holiness, love, healing, and answers will be the hallmarks of this body, this temple, where Christ is Lord.

There are many things to be said about what the Church, the body of Christ, the community of saints, ought to be and will be returned to. I hope what was written here stirs desire in your heart to see this temple in glory and fullness. Still, the building of this collective temple is not the focus of this book, even though it is central, and I am passionate about it. May Christ paint a picture in your own heart of His glorious bride.

Q. In your own words, how would you describe the Babylon you see around you?

_____
_____
_____
_____
_____

Q. God wants to dwell and walk among His people. Describe what that might look like in your personal world.

_____
_____
_____
_____
_____

Q. What does the temple of your life look like today?

_____
_____
_____
_____
_____

Much Rubbish

> Everything God builds, has walls.
> God is by nature, a Divider. -SS

CHAPTER 7

Unprotected

And [I] said unto the king, Let the king live for ever: why should not my countenance be sad, when the city, the place of my fathers' sepulchres, lieth waste, and the gates thereof are consumed with fire?" (Nehemiah 2:3)

Cities without walls are used in Scripture to depict a helpless and defenseless position. Solomon described it as a man with no rule of his own spirit. The New Jerusalem of God is pictured as having high walls and massive gates.

> He that hath no rule over his own spirit is like a city that is broken down, and without walls. (Proverbs 25:28)

Jerusalem was in trouble. Even though the people had returned and had restored sacrifices and praise in a newly built temple, the city itself was not secure. When Nebuchadnezzar conquered Jerusalem, he not only spoiled the temple, but he also burned down the houses and tore holes in the walls. The gates, the means by which the city created safety for its inhabitants, were burned with fire.

*   *   *   *

Johanan woke with a start to muffled sounds in the street. A horse whinnied, and someone gave a yell. Johanan sprang from his bed, grabbed his sword from the wall, and fastened the belt around his waist. Carefully but hurriedly, he fastened sandals on his feet. The rest of his clothes could wait, but the means to run and to fight could not. Lighting his torch from the embers, he ran out into the night.

Havilah waited up for an hour. What did all the yelling and running mean? Was Johanan alright? She gently shushed the little ones back into their peaceful sleep. Johanan returned after more than an hour, drenched with sweat and dirty. He talked as he cleaned up and washed himself. The disturbance had been caused by a small group of rustlers that had broken into the cattle area. One of the shepherds heard them and sounded the alarm. Seeing the torches coming from all sides, the robbers had fled. No one knew where they had gone or who they were. Johanan and other men had given chase, and then turned back to gather the cattle. They lay back down again, but Havilah noticed that Johanan left the sword by the bed. He put out the torch, but he re-wicked it and came to bed with his sandals laced on his feet.

Johanan left early for his office chamber in the temple. Havilah knew there would be meetings all day concerning the nighttime attacks. Something had to be done. Too much was being lost to theft, and some families had even been attacked in their own homes.

Johanan came home early in the afternoon to prepare for the evening sacrifice. He looked too old for his 40 years, and he had dark circles around his eyes. He smiled and touched her kindly, but Havilah knew something was troubling him. Grandpa Joiakim had taken over most of the high priest's duties, although Johanan's father Eliashib was also helping out. Johanan was mostly tasked with hearing the people, listening, and helping find solutions. There was much to do in aiding the people, especially in regard to finding and establishing inheritance.

Later that night, Johanan began to share some of the burden he felt. Havilah was glad, for even though it generated some fears of her own, she felt safer in the connection with her husband.

News was coming in of more atrocities in the area. An entire family had been found murdered in a nearby village. Every day brought new reports of missing livestock from somewhere nearby. Tobiah, whom Great-grandpa Jeshua had despised and marked as an enemy, seemed to be gaining favor with some of the local rulers. There were many letters being passed around.

Moreover in those days the nobles of Judah sent many letters unto Tobiah, and the letters of Tobiah came unto them. (Nehemiah 6:17)

Johanan had his hands full with constant meetings with community leaders and elders and matters of court concerning property. Between all the other things, he also taught in the temple school. This special school was for the children of priests, the exceptionally gifted of the nation, and the scribes.

The local magistrate, a governor serving under King Artaxerxes, didn't seem concerned with the lack of safety. He was very concerned, though, that all the tax money be sent back to Shushan very promptly.

Meanwhile, the nightly raids continued and even worsened.

Johanan and his father Eliashib called the people together to pray for God to show them His great plan for the debacle. Far into the night they prayed.

A thousand miles away, a small visiting procession entered the city of Shushan (Susa, Iran.) Elated to hear news of Jerusalem, Nehemiah, the king's cup-bearer, attended a small gathering of Jews. All of them gathered around the newcomers to hear what had become of the Jews who went back to Jerusalem. Nehemiah listened intently to the stories of the temple with its towering turrets.

But then the stories grew darker as they told of the struggling, the mocking of enemies, the suffering, and the reproach. Cold fingers wrapped around his heart. Unable to contain himself, Nehemiah sank to his knees and wept. Gripped by the pain, the shame, and the hurt of it all, he sobbed far into the night and would not be comforted. The next day and the next, Nehemiah refused to eat. He wept and mourned until only empty eyes remained. He prayed.

> **And it came to pass, when I heard these words, that I sat down and wept, and mourned certain days, and fasted, and prayed before the God of heaven. (Nehemiah 1:4)**

Few people understand the burden of the Word of the Lord. Fewer still will carry that burden. But Nehemiah was one who would, and God knew it. Repentance flowed from his lips as sorrow flowed from his eyes. He bore before the Lord the awfulness of the mistakes of Israel. He reminded the Lord of His own promises. God is not slack concerning His promise. Sometimes, though, we need to remind Him of what He has promised—not because He forgets, but because we do. We need to say them so we believe.

The king watched his cupbearer and taster closely. In the days before Secret Service, it was common for royalty to die in their own house, often killed by someone close to them. Poisoning was one way this was done. To avoid it, the king selected one trustworthy person to serve his wine and taste it and the food he consumed. On this occasion, the cupbearer hesitated. He tested the food and wine, but something was wrong—very wrong. Artaxerxes studied Nehemiah carefully.

> **Wherefore the king said unto me, Why is thy countenance sad, seeing thou art not sick? this is nothing else but sorrow of heart. (Nehemiah 2:2)**

"Wait a minute," said the king. "You aren't afraid. You are sad and heartbroken. You must tell me why."

How does one explain the burden of the deep call and yearning, the cry of the Spirit of God, to a pagan king? Nehemiah did his best, and the king listened. He not only listened, he heard. Artaxerxes' response spoke volumes as he essentially asked, "What do you want?"

The king gave Nehemiah everything he asked for. In Nehemiah's mind, however, it was given not by Artaxerxes, but by God Himself.

> **And the king granted me, according to the good hand of my God upon me. (Nehemiah 2:8b)**

Armed with a commission from the king, an edict to the governor, and a passion to make Jerusalem safe, Nehemiah set out on a journey. No one believed that his mission was possible. Too many roadblocks stood in the way of the walls being built. The political landscape was not favorable. Even some Jews in the city of Jerusalem had alliance with local chiefs who hated God and His people. (Nehemiah 6:10, 17)

Palpable fear surrounded the idea of building the wall. Kings had forbidden the temple works for years; how likely would they be to allow the building of the wall? Physically, it also looked impossible. This job was not an ordinary task for a mason who could take a cartload of stones and lay them into a wall. Far from it. This wall was 16 feet thick, and in some places, it rose 30 to 50 feet straight up from a cliff.

Massive gates needed to be fashioned, by hand of course. Someone had to engineer them. They couldn't buy the hinges from the local hardware store. Blacksmiths had to fashion them by hand, and then the hinges had to be implanted deep into the stone wall so they could support thousands of pounds. The scope of the project was enough to intimidate anyone. Anyone, that is, except a man with a passion from heaven and a mandate from God.

> **Then I told them of the hand of my God which was good upon me; as also the king's words that he had spoken unto me. (Nehemiah 2:18a)**

Why do we live unprotected? I remember waking up one night to the screams of my infant daughter. I struggled out of bed and dashed over to her room. As I picked her up, I discovered something that sent chills up my spine and instantly made me wide awake.

She was asleep.

In her sleep, she was screaming. Even as a young father, I knew what that meant. She was having a horrifying nightmare, seeing torment, feeling fear, and screaming in terror. She couldn't even talk yet. Something evil had come into my house and was tormenting my beautiful, helpless infant daughter.

First, I was horrified. Then I got angry. More feelings flooded over me. The immediate nightmare was not the biggest problem. I woke my daughter, calmed her, and prayed over her until she was comforted. I was not comforted, however. What was coming into my house? Why? Who let it in? How did I fight this...this THING? And why was I unprotected from this sort of harassment?

This event, among others, sent me on a quest for understanding. This book is an attempt to show you some of the answers that I believe God gave us. Far too much time passed, with too much foolishness being worked against my family, before I learned how to fight back. Too many things happened that I would never tolerate today.

It isn't about effort only, or about desire. No one who knew me as a youth will tell you I was careless in the pursuit of God. I lost track of the hours I spent walking the roads and the cornfields of Iowa, deep in the night, weeping and seeking eternal truth. It continued after my marriage. Why am I saying this?

Because walls are not built only by what we want.

Broken down walls leave us open to attack. Over 150 years before Nebuchadnezzar came, and more than 200 years before Nehemiah, the prophet Hosea mourned:

My people are destroyed for lack of knowledge: because thou hast rejected knowledge, I will also reject thee, that thou shalt be no priest to me: seeing thou hast forgotten the law of thy God, I will also forget thy children. (Hosea 4:6)

Today, I see people tormented on all sides. Marriages fail. Children are born out of wedlock. Drug addiction took the life of another beautiful girl as I was writing this chapter. Alcoholism is everywhere. Parents call me because children are screaming in the night or throwing fits at the name of Jesus. Panic attacks threaten lives. There is a plague of youth cutting themselves with razors. Sexual abuse has become rampant. Relationships fracture. Mental illness and depression are medicated, but they continue anyway. Church girls run for abortions. Porn addictions seems normal. A local pastor is found to have two separate families. People are deeply wounded by authority in church life, but they are not healed. Adults who were sexually abused as children remain tormented. Physical diseases with spiritual roots take lives. (Jeremiah 8:22)

Why is this happening?

Is it possible that our walls are broken down? Is it possible that we have grown so used to the enemy's attacks that we consider them part of the Christian life, just "bearing our cross"? Are we being robbed continually by an enemy because we have no gates? Have we so concentrated on building a temple (being born again) that we have lost awareness of walls as protection? Have we relegated all efforts at wall-building to a despised class of dead works?

Do Sanballat and Tobiah, the demons of our culture and society, simply walk into our life and our city as they please? Do they carry on trade there? Have they rented a room in the temple?

Has our godless society influenced our worship? Is the voice of Tobiah respected in the temple of our spirit? Are we suffering robbery at the hands of spirits that hate God and His people? Have our personal lives been compromised by the inability to clearly see and define the enemy? Has the church in the West come into a place of affliction and reproach?

> **And they said unto me, The remnant that are left of the captivity there in the province are in great affliction and reproach: the wall of Jerusalem also is broken down, and the gates thereof are burned with fire. (Nehemiah 1:3)**

> **And I came to Jerusalem, and understood of the evil that Eliashib did for Tobiah, in preparing him a chamber in the courts of the house of God. (Nehemiah 13:7)**

I would say YES, with great weeping and sorrow, to all the above questions. The wall has been broken down, and we are unprotected and suffering unnecessarily. We are suffering as a culture and society, we are suffering as a collective Western Church, and we are suffering individually. The darkness has increased, and that simply means the light has dimmed. Christ, as the LIGHT of the world, never dims, but He has called us the light of this world also. When we fail to reflect with any accuracy the Light He is, then darkness increases.

The darkness comes to kill, steal, and destroy. Christ has come that we might have life, and have it abundantly. Because the walls of our life—the repentance, the restitution, the obedience in detail to the will of the Father—have not been seen as essential to the "goal" of getting to heaven, we have discarded them as useless altogether. But they are not useless. These stones were meant to build a wall for our protection against the enemies of the living God, the fiends of darkness.

Failure to build up the walls is an inadvertent invitation to the darkness.

I will do these things unto thee, because thou hast gone a whoring after the heathen, and because thou art polluted with their idols. (Ezekiel 23:30)

Q. What three areas of your life do you see as being unprotected?

_____
_____
_____
_____
_____

Q. What areas of your church appear to be unprotected?

_____
_____
_____
_____
_____

Q. Name some specific things you see in culture that have been overrun by evil and darkness, as though there is little light.

_____
_____
_____
_____
_____

> **Walls are built to stop assault. That which hates the wall, is always the enemy.** -SS

CHAPTER 8

Building the Wall

Building the walls is hard work. In the words of Jesus, it isn't good to build a tower without sitting down to count the cost and see if there is enough to finish it. Starting to build a wall or tower without consideration to cost will open you to mockery by the very enemies whose harassment you want to stop.

> **And whosoever doth not bear his cross, and come after me, cannot be my disciple. For which of you, intending to build a tower, sitteth not down first, and counteth the cost, whether he have sufficient to finish it? Lest haply, after he hath laid the foundation, and is not able to finish it, all that behold it begin to mock him, Saying, This man began to build, and was not able to finish. (Luke 14:27-30)**

As Jesus was so aptly pointing out, the very first element in building defenses against the enemy is absolute surrender to the Lord God. This concept is often referred to by Jesus as taking up the cross. It is further reinforced in Revelation:

And they overcame him by the blood of the Lamb, and by the word of their testimony; and they loved not their lives unto the death. (Revelation 12:11)

In both the examples that Jesus referenced in Luke 14, the concept was DEFENSIVE. According to *Strong's Concordance*, the biblical definition of a tower is "A fortified structure rising to considerable height, to repel hostile attacks or enable a watchman to see in every direction."

Jesus also gave an example of being attacked by a larger force. The WALL of defense is important in God's economy. People who laugh and claim all superior power as their own and become careless are dangerous and should be avoided. Christ has not bid us walk in fear, but neither has He called us to walk in stupidity. Walls have a purpose in our lives, much as they did in Jerusalem of old. Spiritual defenses need to be raised around us both personally and corporately to make a safe environment from the evil beings that would torment and harangue us. Our children deserve a protection that many of us did not experience and find hard to visualize. Furthermore, there is another purpose for a wall in addition to safety.

* * * *

Johanan lay back in the hammock and groaned ever so slightly. He was grateful that God had set aside a day each week for rest. His family had always treated the Sabbath and the law surrounding it very seriously. Today, Johanan was glad for it because he was spent.

Havilah was resting inside. Several of the children chattered over a game nearby, and the oldest two sons were at a meeting with other students in the temple. Scenes from the last months passed through Johanan's memory. He contemplated the break-ins, the fear, the political pushing, and the losses. One of the local families had even lost a daughter to a raiding band of Philistines from the south.

Johanan recalled the meeting where Hanani and five others were commissioned to go to Shushan the palace. They had been given the best horses and all the necessary supplies for the 1,000-mile trip. Several months later, a rider had galloped into Jerusalem on the back of a lathered horse. Fearing the worst, Johanan had rushed out of his temple office with the nobles, and they all had gathered at the entrance to wait.

The rider sprang from his horse and gasped, "He's coming!" Snatching at the skin of water offered him, he drank deeply before continuing, "Nehemiah is on his way to Jerusalem and will arrive tomorrow. I left the group this morning to tell you."

The story tumbled out quickly. Nehemiah was Hanani's brother, and he had stayed behind in Shushan. Nehemiah was bold and fierce, and he had the ear of Artaxerxes, being the king's cupbearer. The commission from Jerusalem had met Nehemiah, who fell to his face in agony and weeping when he heard of conditions in Jerusalem.

When the king learned the reason for Nehemiah's grief, he sent him back to Jerusalem to do what he could for his nation. Now Nehemiah was on his way with an entourage of the Persian guard. Not only that, but he was coming as governor, appointed by the king himself.

Johanan had heard enough. Unconscious of the stares, he broke from his position and headed for his house at a lope. Havilah was startled when he appeared at midday, out of breath and nearly in tears.

"He's coming!" Johanan choked. Then seeing his wife's puzzled face, he collected himself and continued more calmly, "Remember how we prayed for a man with answers? He's on his way here as our new governor."

Havilah sank into a chair as the weight of the news settled on her. "You mean ..." her voice trailed off.

"Yes," said her husband softly.

Johanan took his sons with him to prepare a suite in the temple for Nehemiah. They set up a bed to serve for a long-term stay and arranged for food to be delivered and prepared.

Now Johanan shifted in the hammock as he recalled the scene when Nehemiah's procession came around the Mount of Olives and toward the gate. Nehemiah had sat motionless on his horse, taking in the temple and the city, defenseless without walls. He dismounted and came toward Johanan. His eyes were steel. His shoulders were straight. There was no give or intimidation in this man. Determination fairly screamed from his carriage, and has handshake declared purpose.

They shared dinner that night and talked. It was good—very good—Johanan thought. Still, he knew in his heart that something huge was going on that he didn't yet understand.

"He's hiding something," Havilah told him that night. "Nehemiah isn't telling us everything."

Several days had passed while the countryside buzzed with the news that the region had a new governor, and a Jew at that. Swift riders carrying letters came and went. The marketplace was full of groups discussing this man, Nehemiah. Sanballat and Tobiah, the local mob bosses, were absolutely livid. But Johanan smirked when he remembered how the captain of the Persian guards had responded to Sanballat. He left no doubt about who was in charge and who would be obeyed.

Then that fateful night . . . Nehemiah had pulled Johanan aside after the evening sacrifice.

"Tonight, meet me by the valley gate, mounted." It was a deja-vu moment, Johanan realized, as he rode out of the city behind the princely man in white hair.

In the darkness of that evening, Johanan rode in silence with Nehemiah and three others. They spent several hours riding around the city while Nehemiah took careful notes. When they had finished, they stabled their horses and gathered in a temple chamber. The air was tense with expectation as everyone looked expectantly at Nehemiah.

His words fell like thunder, piercing through the darkness. "WE ARE GOING TO BUILD THE WALL!"

Then said I unto them, Ye see the distress that we are in, how Jerusalem lieth waste, and the gates thereof are burned with fire: come, and let us build up the wall of Jerusalem, that we be no more a reproach. Then I told them of the hand of my God which was good upon me; as also the king's words that he had spoken unto me. And they said, Let us rise up and build. So they strengthened their hands for this good work. (Nehemiah 2:17, 18)

Johanan remembered vividly his initial feelings of that night. Build the wall? It was impossible. Too many people were afraid of Sanballat. Tobiah had a room in the temple. Johanan could lose everything he owned just for trying to help! But Nehemiah went on, telling about the burden, the tears, and the hand of God on him.

Slowly, as the sun rose, hope rose with it. Still, the first steps had been as awful as Johanan had feared. Sanballat and Tobiah openly mocked the plan in the market the following day. Some of the nobles sided with them. Others were simply afraid and stayed silent, declining to declare allegiance to either side. But silence had fallen as Nehemiah walked up to the mockers, the Persian captain at his side. Nehemiah marched up to Sanballat, raised his voice, and sternly commanded him to leave.

"God is going to prosper us!" he fairly shouted. "You don't belong here at all. You have no history or future here. We will build. You will get out." (Nehemiah 2:20)

And just like that, the current had shifted. Courage rose as people stepped forward to throw in their lot with Nehemiah. Riders went out in all directions, summoning help from other areas. Nehemiah and his assistants ordered materials from the king's forest. They organized the massive food preparation that was needed to feed the workmen. Nehemiah's group alone consumed one cow, six sheep, and many chickens each day!

Now that which was prepared for me daily was one ox and six choice sheep; also fowls were prepared for me, and once in ten days store of all sorts of wine: yet for all this required not I the bread of the governor, because the bondage was heavy upon this people. (Nehemiah 5:18)

Johanan remembered the early morning his father Eliashib came knocking and said, "I need you and your sons today."

That day, Eliashib and Johanan had stepped forward and begun to build. That had been two weeks ago, Johanan now realized. No wonder he was so tired. Two weeks of running, pulling, lifting, organizing, and fighting.

Johanan lifted his arm to see how his arrow wound was healing. It seemed fine. Havilah, of course, was less than impressed when he came home with a broken arrow protruding from his arm. But the wound was healing nicely now.

The building had started out so well. Nehemiah, it seemed, never slept. Before daylight, he was riding the wall. As men awoke, he shouted encouragement to them over their breakfast.

All the organization and frustration fell to him all day long. Some of the nobles of the Tekoites refused to help, but the people did their part.

> **And next unto them the Tekoites repaired; but their nobles put not their necks to the work of their Lord. (Nehemiah 3:5)**

Then the harassment started. Sanballat and his cronies stood by and made snide remarks at first, then progressed to open mockery. They tried to get Nehemiah to meet with them outside the city. He asked Johanan to pray about their invitation, and they subsequently refused to meet as requested.

Johanan had felt a little strange the first day he carried his sword to work. Several others saw it and returned home for theirs also. Something evil was in the air, and he felt it. Nehemiah, riding by, saw it too. He knew the Arabians, Ammonites, and Ashdodites were angry as hornets. (Nehemiah 4:7)

Sure enough, that afternoon they had attacked. The yells of the fighting attracted the whole builders' brigade. Hammers, rocks, chisels, and trowels filled the air. Johanan pulled his sword. Seeing the steel, the band of attackers fled, but not before some laborers were wounded. Johanan had taken an arrow in the arm.

As he reflected, tiredness took its toll, and Johanan drifted off to sleep. He started up suddenly at the shaking of his hammock. Nehemiah was there, accompanied by several strangers from the countryside.

"Listen to them," Nehemiah urged.

The older man pulled his face kerchief down. He looked into Johanan's eyes and said slowly, "From whatever place you turn, they will be coming." He repeated the line ten times for emphasis. And then they were gone. (Nehemiah 4:12)

The next weeks were brutal. Attacks came from every side. Nehemiah, though, stayed calm and operated brilliantly. He had a few guards hiding inside strategic places with bows and spears. Watchers were assigned to patrol the wall. When they spotted the enemy, the watchmen sounded trumpets. At the sound, the archers emerged, firing arrows. By the time the enemy got close enough to fight, they faced too big a force and retreated.

Therefore set I in the lower places behind the wall, and on the higher places, I even set the people after their families with their swords, their spears, and their bows ... In what place therefore ye hear the sound of the trumpet, resort ye thither unto us: our God shall fight for us. (Nehemiah 4:13, 20)

Nehemiah and the other men agreed together to take watches in the night, for attacks came even then. They never removed their clothes or swords except for bathing. It was a brutal month, but the hardest part of all was the discouragement of those doing the heavy work. Before a solid wall could be built, the rubble had to be removed all the way down to a solid foundation.

It is DEMORALZING to have to sort through what WAS, to find solid footing for what will be a wall.

> **And Judah said, The strength of the bearers of burdens is decayed, and there is much rubbish; so that we are not able to build the wall. (Nehemiah 4:10)**
>
> **THERE WAS MUCH RUBBISH.**

As we noted in the last chapter, many today have built a temple in their personal life. Yet they experience extreme suffering and theft of their possessions and inheritance. We have grown used to the oppression and fear. In this condition, one would hardly think seriously about rebuilding walls. The Sanballats and Tobiahs of shame, accusation, and ridicule sneer from the sidelines. Fear and accusation, though, stand ready to "help" if we are foolish enough to accept their offer. Shame has rented its own room in the temple.

We need a Nehemiah.

Somewhere, someone must weep before the Lord until a vision of true freedom and dominion is birthed. This reality . . . in YOU . . . must have a vision from heaven and a determination not of human origin. This vision, this belief, this faith, this inner power—only this will sustain you when even the "nobles" within are ready to quit. When the chips are down and you discover things inside the walls that ought not be there, anger must rise up against it. You will address all that is noble or ruling in you, and you will turn the tide of public opinion. You will do it by consulting yourself.

> **And I was very angry when I heard their cry and these words. Then I consulted with myself, and I rebuked the nobles, and the rulers, and said unto them, Ye exact usury, every one of his brother. And I set a great assembly against them. (Nehemiah 5:6, 7)**

All this will take place even as the enemy attacks from without. But the greatest struggle you will face is the temptation to quit. There is just TOO MUCH RUBBISH.

Do I have your permission to speak plainly? My little girl screamed in the night because she was being attacked. I fought very hard against the attacks until one day it occurred to me that they shouldn't be happening at all!

I could not imagine them away.

I could not wish them away.

I could not command them away.

My armor didn't stop them from attacking my girl. But I could fix the hole in the wall where the attackers were shooting in. It was very hard work. It was dirty, sweaty labor. First, I had to find where the breach was. Next, I had to determine how the damage to the wall had occurred. Then, fighting discouragement and direct, personal, demonic attacks, I began to dig through the rubble for a solid foundation. And guess what?

THERE WAS MUCH RUBBISH.

The wall that was damaged was in a section of my life labelled "Information." The breach was caused by some past involvement with the occult. The problem was, I didn't know what that meant or how to find it. I pulled out stones of truth that were covered with manmade mortar. I chiseled off the mortar, then set the stone carefully off to the side to be reused. I dug through the rubble of my past. I sifted through garbage in my wife's life, then my parents. I searched Scripture and read books. THERE WAS MUCH RUBBISH. My strength decayed, and the attacks increased until I was nearly drowning in depression. I wept night and day until I could scarcely function. Still, my girls suffered while I slowly learned. I began to see the solid foundations of eternal reality. Hope rose once more. I began, with some help, to repent of one sin after another along with my wife. Stones of repentance were placed on the foundations of apostles and prophets, and then stones of truth were cemented in. Large stones of truth were lugged up by small cranes. All the wall was plastered with love.

For behold this selfsame thing, that ye sorrowed after a godly sort, what carefulness it wrought in you, yea, what clearing of yourselves, yea, what indignation, yea, what fear, yea, what vehement desire, yea, what zeal, yea, what revenge! In all things ye have approved yourselves to be clear in this matter. (2 Corinthians 7:11)

At the time, I didn't know Paul had laid it out so clearly. But suddenly, the attacks stopped. I waited ... and waited ... and then I realized that breach was gone! THAT wall was built. My wife was healed, my girls were safe, and I was filled with vehement zeal! Finally, I felt real hope and real freedom and real power for the future.

If only I had known then that there were other walls with their own breaches, and that gates needed to be hung. There were broken walls of immorality. There was a huge gap in the wall of accusation. Shame was speaking in the temple. The wall of peace was missing sections, and the tower of acceptance was crumbling. It can be built up again. Real freedom from these attacks can happen. The arrows stop. Victory comes, not when you shoot more arrows at the enemy, but when he can no longer shoot at you!

But THERE IS MUCH RUBBISH.
Build the wall. Rise up, find men to help you, and build the wall! Fight. Dig through the rubbish of what you have been taught. Save the good stones though—you'll need them to build with.

Most people fail in sorting the actual stone of truth from rubbish.

They also often fail in continuing to dig for SOLID foundation. Find the truth, and tie it about your neck.

Building the wall took only 52 days. (Nehemiah 6:15, 16)

The enemy fears your wall.

Q. In Johanan's story, why do you think the wall had never been built? What were the main reasons?

_____
_____
_____
_____
_____

Q. What are areas of your life that are under attack? Where do you struggle and fail too often?

_____
_____
_____
_____
_____

Q. If the enemies could not attack that area of your life at all, what would life look like for you going forward?

_____
_____
_____
_____
_____

Much Rubbish

> **Every structure of value must have a foundation. Foundations, to have value, must never move. -SS**

CHAPTER 9

Uncovering Foundation

This Ezra went up from Babylon; and he was a ready scribe in the law of Moses, which the Lord God of Israel had given: and the king granted him all his request, according to the hand of the Lord his God upon him. (Ezra 7:6)

Johanan stood quietly off to the side, watching Ezra write. Zechariah was in the temple today after spending the night in prayer. When he spoke, it was as the oracles of heaven; the words moved something inside those who listened. Ezra, the wise old scribe and priest, had brought out a clean Egyptian papyrus and ink. His quill moved carefully as he recorded the words.

The room smelled of the incense burning in the inner chamber. The sounds of the bustling market and playing children drifted in from the street. Johanan moved off to attend to someone who had come into the temple with a request. He felt privileged to spend time with these patriarchs. Ezra sat down often with Haggai and Zechariah. Hearing the Word of the Lord was very important, as was learning, and teaching. Student and teachers studied together here, often in pairs. Scrolls were carefully preserved in the temple and copied by hand, as they were rare.

Johanan remembered that spot by the River Chebar from his boyhood. Under the trees that lined the water, the children of captivity had met to pray. Sometimes, Ezekiel would show up with his flowing white beard. He would sit quietly for hours, staring at the water before he began to speak gently. Sometimes he wept as he spoke.

With the passing of the years, Johanan had forgotten much of what Ezekiel had said. Ezra, though, had a copy of many of the visions and words of Ezekiel. Johanan still remembered the feelings from those occasions when he listened to the old prophet speak, and now these moments with Ezra, Haggai, and Zechariah in the temple felt like those privileged moments from his boyhood.

He recalled too, the day there in Tel Abil, when Belteshazzar, one of the king's Presidents, showed up on horseback. He came to the river and sat with the people while Ezekiel spoke. Belteshazzar was accompanied by three men who sat with him. He also had a royal guard, but the soldiers stayed some distance away. The President was very kind and took time to speak to each person at the gathering.

Johanan still remembered how President Belteshazzar, also a Jew, had looked into Johanan's eyes as he had said, "Always do the right thing. Honor the law of God, and He will honor you."

Those words had impacted him. They came to mean even more when word spread several years later that President Belteshazzar (Daniel) had been thrown into the lions' pit, but the LORD had delivered him.

Ezra had arrived in Jerusalem some years before with a huge contingent of people and livestock and loaded with wealth. Johanan helped the people find land and destinations according to their inheritance and their fathers. He also helped with the measuring, recording, and storage of the $140 million in gold that Ezra had brought, although the primary responsibility for that was on Great-uncle Jozabad.

Now on the fourth day was the silver and the gold and the vessels weighed in the house of our God by the hand of Meremoth the son of Uriah the priest; and with him was Eleazar the son of Phinehas; and with them was Jozabad the son of Jeshua, and Noadiah the son of Binnui, Levites; By number and by weight of every one: and all the weight was written at that time. (Ezra 8:33, 34)

Johanan quickly learned that Ezra was no simple man. Conscious of the fortune in gold and silver they carried, he had led the entire group in a three-day fast before they began their journey to Jerusalem. They then set out on their journey, believing that God Who blessed them would also protect them.

When Johanan told Ezra about the shady political dealings and the intermarriages with heathen, Ezra was completely horrified. While Johanan watched in astonishment, Ezra pulled out the hair of his head and his beard. Still in public, he tore his garments, then took off his turban and ripped it up too in front of the crowd that had gathered by then. Ezra sat on the ground, lifted up his voice, and wailed in grief. (Ezra 9:3)

At the evening sacrifice, Ezra approached the altar as Johanan and Eliashib offered the sacrifice. He spread his hands, fell on his knees, and prayed. The memory of that prayer still shook Johanan.

And [I] said, O my God, I am ashamed and blush to lift up my face to thee, my God: for our iniquities are increased over our head, and our trespass is grown up unto the heavens. Since the days of our fathers have we been in a great trespass unto this day; and for our iniquities have we, our kings, and our priests, been delivered into the hand of the kings of the lands, to the sword, to captivity, and to a spoil, and to confusion of face, as

it is this day. **And now for a little space grace hath been shewed from the Lord our God, to leave us a remnant to escape, and to give us a nail in his holy place, that our God may lighten our eyes, and give us a little reviving in our bondage. (Ezra 9:6-8)**

People seemed to come from everywhere until a great crowd filled the plaza. Something very strange, very holy, filled the air. From up near the altar, a weeping began. It spread through the crowd until the very walls rang with the sound of it. (Ezra 10:1)

That night, all the priests and elders swore to Ezra that they would complete the work of separating from the heathen of the land. Ezra stumbled into the bedroom suite in Johanan's office afterward, refusing to eat. For several days he wept, prayed, and fasted in that room.

Then Ezra rose up from before the house of God, and went into the chamber of Johanan the son of Eliashib: and when he came thither, he did eat no bread, nor drink water: for he mourned because of the transgression of them that had been carried away. (Ezra 10:6)

Messages were sent to all cities and corners of the land, summoning the people to a solemn assembly. Everyone MUST come or face excommunication and forfeiture of all property. The people came in response to the summons. They repented, even in the rain. That was the day Johanan began to truly comprehend the nature of FOUNDATIONS. Sure, he had been quite young when the foundations of the temple were laid. He remembered the earthshaking shout and cry from that celebration. He had worked until his hands bled to uncover the foundation of the wall. But now, he understood FOUNDATION.

* * * *

Building a good foundation is hard work. It takes time, lots of digging, and effort. Under the temple wall in Jerusalem, for example, lies a large rock called the Western Stone that makes up part of the foundation. It is one of the biggest cut stones in the world and is visible from a tunnel beside it. It is 44 feet long, 10 feet high, and about 10 feet thick. Its weight is estimated at 517 tons. No one knows why a stone of that magnitude was used there by the builders. What is obvious, though, is that they understood the concept of solid foundations. We don't even know how the builders managed the incredible feat of moving the Western Stone into position.

> **If the foundations be destroyed, what can the righteous do? (Psalm 11:3)**

The prophet Ezekiel, mourning in captivity close to Babylon, bemoaned the walls built by man. Not only was the wall built falsely, it was daubed with mortar that was untempered. God promised to bring down the wall, uncover the foundation, and consume those who built it.

Because, even because they have seduced my people, saying, Peace; and there was no peace; and one built up a wall, and, lo, others daubed it with untempered morter: Say unto them which daub it with untempered morter, that it shall fall: there shall be an overflowing shower; and ye, O great hailstones, shall fall; and a stormy wind shall rend it. Lo, when the wall is fallen, shall it not be said unto you, Where is the daubing wherewith ye have daubed it? Therefore thus saith the Lord God; I will even rend it with a stormy wind in my fury; and there shall be an overflowing shower in mine anger, and great hailstones in my fury to consume it. So will I break down the wall that ye have daubed with untempered morter, and bring

it down to the ground, so that the foundation thereof shall be discovered, and it shall fall, and ye shall be consumed in the midst thereof: and ye shall know that I am the Lord. Thus will I accomplish my wrath upon the wall, and upon them that have daubed it with untempered morter, and will say unto you, The wall is no more, neither they that daubed it; To wit, the prophets of Israel which prophesy concerning Jerusalem, and which see visions of peace for her, and there is no peace, saith the Lord God. (Ezekiel 13:10-16)

This seems to focus particularly on those who prophesied "peace, peace" when in fact destruction was coming. The prophecy was built on an entirely wrong premise. This theme of solid foundations is picked up in the New Testament also. Paul says that the foundation is Jesus Christ, and again, the apostles and prophets with Jesus Christ as Chief Cornerstone.

> **For other foundation can no man lay than that is laid, which is Jesus Christ. (1 Corinthians 3:11)**
>
> **And are built upon the foundation of the apostles and prophets, Jesus Christ himself being the chief corner stone. (Ephesians 2:20)**

He then further instructs us to be very careful how we build on the foundation and what sort of building material we use.

According to the grace of God which is given unto me, as a wise masterbuilder, I have laid the foundation, and another buildeth thereon…But let every man take heed how he buildeth thereupon. Now if any man build upon this foundation gold, silver, precious stones, wood, hay, stubble; Every man's work shall be made manifest: for the day shall declare it, because it shall be revealed by fire; and the fire shall try every man's work of what sort it is. (1 Corinthians 3:10, 12, 13)

Nor was Paul alone in using this word picture. Jesus likened someone who hears the Word, and DOES it, to someone who dug deep and laid their foundation on a rock. Those who hear but do not DO anything in response are building on a cheap foundation of earth. (Luke 6:47-49)

The writer of Hebrews tells us that repentance from dead works and faith toward God is in the foundation of what we believe. Abraham looked for a city that has foundations, whose builder and maker is God. When God builds, He understands foundations. In Revelation, the holy Jerusalem is pictured as coming down from God. It has 12 foundations:

And the wall of the city had twelve foundations, and in them the names of the twelve apostles of the Lamb. (Revelation 21:14)

In the last chapter, we spoke of building walls. One of the most difficult and disheartening things was that THERE WAS MUCH RUBBISH. Rubbish is wall material, misplaced and collapsed. It includes the stones used before, the mortar, and broken material no longer useable. All of this material must be SORTED out. Things of no value may be discarded and thrown over a cliff. The foundation MUST be uncovered. If, however, in the process of sorting, real stones are rolled over the edge and discarded, what will you use to build your wall?

Sorting through the debris between rocks and rubbish, finding all loose stones and removing them right down to the foundations, is what decays strength. Picture yourself on the edge of a cliff with the valley below. You are building a wall here, so that even if the enemy climbs the cliff from below, he will still face a wall. The wall is broken down now, so you must dig for the foundations.

The easiest thing to do is simply to throw all the pieces into the valley below. Watching those square cut rocks bounce down the cliff is kind of fun. Finally, you get to solid material to build upon. Good. Now, what will you build in the gap? At this point, you realize you actually needed those stones. So, you traipse around the edge of the hill, down the steep trail to the valley. There, you realize how heavy the rocks really are. You can scarcely lift them by yourself. Suddenly it dawns on you that it will take an entire lifetime to lug these stones back up the hill. You haven't the strength to face it, much less actually do it.

And so your city lies unprotected. How much better would it have been to sort carefully through the rubbish? You could have kept that which had value and built it back on the foundation properly. Most failure happens, though, from MUCH RUBBISH.

I am speaking in pictures because they are broad and cover all of life. Let me give some practical examples, but please, please don't get hung up on them alone. My little girls were being tormented at night. The "information" section of my wall had a huge hole in it. Demonic things shot "fiery darts" at my babies through those gaps in the wall. The wall had been broken down, as they always are, by disobedience. An enemy king of divination pulled them down. In case you don't understand, divination is the attempt to get information by accessing the underworld. I had done it, by my own involvement in water witching or dowsing. My wife's youthful involvement in divination had included seances, meetings where demons are summoned to appear. Both of us had some things from Native American religions in our background as well.

The wall was broken.

We were being harassed.

Very carefully, the RUBBISH is sorted. That which is of evil is discarded, repented of, and renounced. This includes the seance, the power it gives, and even the desire for it. It includes the water witching, the desire for that sort of information, and the drive to protect it. It also included the reaching out and TOUCHING of the unclean.

Wherefore come out from among them, and be ye separate, saith the Lord, and touch not the unclean thing; and I will receive you. (2 Corinthians 6:17)

This word "unclean" is *akarthortos* in Greek, and it carries a primary meaning of relating to the demonic.

However, among the rubbish we also find solid stones. We DO need to recognize the spirit world exists. We do need true things, and we do need correct information. We should worship. There is healing in Christ. The Holy Spirit does operate today. The Bible IS right.

And so, by repentance, we disposed of the rubbish. By recognizing and declaring TRUTH, we built the wall. The attacks stopped. And today, if something tries to climb that wall, it meets a violent response from me.

*   *   *   *

A girl grows up in a churchgoing family, albeit one that is somewhat dysfunctional. At 16, she is tired of all the arrows piercing her through the wrecked walls of her parents' lives. So in defiance of the King of the city, she throws all the stuff from the walls over the edge. She chooses to ignore the temple, and instead parties with the enemies of God.

Years later, she wants to return and comes to my office for help. I try to help her clean out the temple and establish worship there. It takes time and much work. But when it comes to the walls, I scarcely know what to do. Some of the walls lie broken beyond repair. There is much rubbish. I will do my best to help her, but after 30 relationships, multiple diseases, several abortions, and two fatherless children, it will take an entire generation to fix some of the walls. Some of them take years of hard labor to establish. They can be trashed in a moment and lost over the cliff of carelessness, from which there is no return.

If the walls had been respected and repaired, they would provide a lifetime of relative safety. Furthermore, the blessing of that wall might be passed on for the benefit of the children. But once thrown down and the stones lobbed over the cliff, there will inevitably be loss. Also, there will be continued, needless attacks, and they will pass to our children

---

For ye know how that afterward, when he would have inherited the blessing, he was rejected: for he found no place of repentance, though he sought it carefully with tears. (Hebrews 12:17)

Be not deceived; God is not mocked: for whatsoever a man soweth, that shall he also reap. (Galatians 6:7)

So much suffering occurs today among God's people because we have disregarded walls. What should be a life of clarity and dominion over evil becomes a fight for survival instead. Where milk and honey should be the norm, people settle instead for mere existence. Those whose walls are shattered can be brought into a corporate place where walls are maintained. There, they enjoy some of the safety of the walls others have built. Still, a lifetime of sorting through rubbish will be necessary, and many times, we simply run out of strength

*　　*　　*　　*

An Amish man finds a genuine experience of Christ within. He leaves to worship God and hear His voice. In other words, he builds a temple. Eventually, he and his family decide to exit the Amish ways. He has correctly determined that many of the walls of his past lie in shambles, and he is far too vulnerable to shots from the evil one. Disgusted at the attempts of his predecessors to build walls, he faces a daunting challenge. He has three basic choices:

> 1. Focus on the temple and ignore the walls completely. Roll the stones over the cliff with the rubbish. You might find the foundations, and only foundations matter in today's world anyway.

Problem: he will live defenseless from evil. Sanbballat and Tobiah will have general sway over his life. They will provide a measure of "freedom and safety" as long as they are obeyed.

> **Know ye not, that to whom ye yield yourselves servants to obey, his servants ye are to whom ye obey; whether of sin unto death, or of obedience unto righteousness? (Romans 6:16)**

2. Write everything off and start all over again. Level all the walls and forget worship.

Problem: the sin, rebellion against God, and disobedience will get him a trip back to Babylon.

3. Worship in the temple, but restore walls. Sort through the debris, keep all stones of value, and throw out the trash. Rebuild the wall.

Problem: There is much RUBBISH. It is very long, hard work. The demonic realm, sensing it is about to be trounced, will fight, attack, lie, and cheat. It is tough to pull off.

The third one is the most difficult. It is also the correct choice.

The man sees heaps of buggies, black clothes, rules, bonnets, horse-drawn equipment, and restrictions. One element at a time, he has to sort through it all. He must discard the excess details of man while carefully keeping all the principles and realities of God. If he keeps too much manmade debris, it will frustrate him and weaken the wall. If he throws away what he should have kept, it will prevent him from building the wall back again. There is much rubbish.

Under each wall, there is a foundation. That foundation goes back a LONG way. It takes a lot of work to uncover, and while doing that, to save the material you need to rebuild.

The foundation you uncover must be solid. The CORE principles of divine reality based on the nature of Jesus Christ and revealed in Scriptures will NOT move. You need to uncover, understand, and build on these unchangeable foundations. This is the only way to build a wall and a life that can operate in true dominion. As this man digs, he will find the bedrock principle of God's holiness. That foundation cannot move or be moved.

Perhaps years of accumulated human notions, ideas, and perspectives have yielded a wall that is in shambles. But the wall needs to be there. The foundation is solid, and the material is good. Chip off the manmade ideas, but keep the stones of separation from the world and of a life of victory and holiness. You must build this wall up in your life. These elements of the true, the honest, the lovely, and good report must be built up if you want a life of dominion. You have to apply these elements in your life. Staring at the foundational truth that God is holy will not protect anything; the stones must be applied to the foundation.

Memorizing Scripture, focusing on character, or applying stones to your wall will not save your soul. That occurs in the temple. We are speaking here of building a life that is useful. Never confuse the building of walls, or of doing right, with salvation. We build walls BECAUSE we have a temple.

Whosoever therefore shall break one of these least commandments, and shall teach men so, he shall be called the least in the kingdom of heaven: but whosoever shall do and teach them, the same shall be called great in the kingdom of heaven. (Matthew 5:19)

The New Testament does not endorse the notion of people running about like cities with no walls, seeking more power. Other than the 70 disciples Jesus sent out for a short while to do miracles, there are no miracles done by wall-less people or by the undeveloped and unprepared. The church, as well as the writers of the Epistles, focused instead on building a LIFE of victory that reflected well on the Savior. The miracles simply follow those who believe. The disrespect for foundations and for living a life of dominion is the work of Tobiah. This enemy of God has rented a room in the temple. People hear his voice and think it is God speaking. But he speaks lies. He needs to be cast out, but first, we need walls. First, we need to uncover foundations.

Then I contended with the nobles of Judah, and said unto them, What evil thing is this that ye do, and profane the sabbath day? Did not your fathers thus, and did not our God bring all this evil upon us, and upon this city? yet ye bring more wrath upon Israel by profaning the sabbath. And it came to pass, that when the gates of Jerusalem began to be dark before the sabbath, I commanded that the gates should be shut, and charged that they should not be opened till after the sabbath: and some of my servants set I at the gates, that there should no burden be brought in on the sabbath day. (Nehemiah 13:17-19)

Q. The FOUNDATIONS that God lays cannot be moved. What are some of those foundations? Can you think of another word for foundations?

_____

_____

_____

_____

_____

Q. What do you see in the world around you that is NOT built on the foundations of God, and will certainly crumble?

_____

_____

_____

_____

_____

Q. Sorting through things from our past life, experiences, and teaching requires a lot of work and a high degree of honesty. What are some things you need to sort through?

_____

_____

_____

_____

_____

Much Rubbish

> "When repentance is once again treasured, freedom will become a way of life." -SS

CHAPTER 10

Repentance

Johanan took his place on the wall beside the other priests. The scene before him took his breath away. All the days and weeks of preparation were paying off at last. Thousands upon thousands of people lined the streets and continued to stream in from the countryside in every direction. Nehemiah was giving orders from his house, with a trumpeter standing nearby. There were also rows of trumpeters lined up while other instrumentalists tuned up and another orchestra gathered on the opposite wall. Hilarity filled the air, and children laughed and shouted. Small groups of women talked and laughed animatedly. Huge vats of food were already starting to cook over open fires. Still, people continued pouring into the city.

Slowly, all the participants found their places; singers, priests, and instrumentalists. Nehemiah certainly had a gift for organizing, Johanan noted again. His officers worked tirelessly, organizing the crowd. With Ezra beside him, Nehemiah motioned for silence. Johanan glanced over at Zechariah, who was holding his trumpet. Zechariah grinned at him, and tears suddenly welled up in Johanan's eyes. Nehemiah gave a signal, and it began.

First the trumpets, pointing in every direction, split the air. Then the cymbals broke out and soon established a rhythm. The people clapped along, and the choir of five thousand voices began the praise songs. The lyres joined in, but the sound of shouting, singing, and trumpets rejoicing together was overwhelming. The children stood in thousands in the streets, awestruck by the color, the arrangements, and the praise. Johanan looked over at his own sons with pride, grateful that they were part of this historic moment and knowing they would never be the same.

Also that day they offered great sacrifices, and rejoiced: for God had made them rejoice with great joy: the wives also and the children rejoiced: so that the joy of Jerusalem was heard even afar off. (Nehemiah 12:43)

Later, Johanan walked through the crowd of joyful worshippers to a parapet on the wall and leaned against it. He gazed down on the crowds, the shouting, the worship, and the sacrifices blazing on the altar in front of the temple. He wished Great-grandpa Jeshua could have been there.

In an instant, Johanan's memory carried him to another gathering, years earlier. The walls were still wrecked, the gates burned, and the temple a heap. An impressionable youth, Johanan stood by the large platform where Ezra held the scroll. Great-grandpa Jeshua stood beside him, along with Zechariah.

Ezra began to read.

Something shifted in the air. A heavy weight fell on the

young Johanan. He glanced around and saw others sinking to the ground. The reading stopped, and a Levite nearby began to explain through tears the meaning of what they had heard. More reading followed, and then Jeshua spoke some more about its meaning. The crowd lost all sense of time. For three hours, they remained transfixed as the weight of the law descended upon them. Much of it Johanan had never heard before. Righteous, holy fear gripped him, as tears began to fall. No wonder they had been subjected to Babylon.

Weeping became a wail, as people felt the weight of their sin and transgressing of God's law. In tears, with their faces to the ground, they worshipped.

> **And Ezra blessed the Lord, the great God. And all the people answered, Amen, Amen, with lifting up their hands: and they bowed their heads, and worshipped the Lord with their faces to the ground. (Nehemiah 8:6)**

Then suddenly Nehemiah, still a young man in those days, had stepped forward.

"No!" he thundered. "No! Up on your feet." Johanan remembered how he had stood, shocked, with the rest of the multitude.

"This day is holy unto the Lord! The joy of the Lord is your strength!" Nehemiah cried.

> **Then he said unto them, Go your way, eat the fat, and drink the sweet, and send portions unto them for whom nothing is prepared: for this day is holy unto our Lord: neither be ye sorry; for the joy of the Lord is your strength. (Nehemiah 8:10)**

And from the midst of the sorrow, joy sprang up. The rest of that day was a sweet time of rejoicing. Even now, Johanan smiled as he remembered dancing in the street with the children around the singers of Psalms.

For seven days after that, the feast had continued. The priests read more of the Law of Moses, and the people built temporary booths of branches. And then that heavy day, twenty-three days later. Once again, Ezra had read the law for three hours. The people were on their faces, repenting and worshipping, for three more days.

Johanan remembered the torn clothing of sacks on all sides. Even though he was young, he had fasted for days with cold ashes from the firepit on his head as a sign of morning. His father Eliashib had piled dirt on his own head, moaning in grief. The deep wailing of men and women had filled the air around him.

For hours they stood, led by a group of priests, and confessed their sins. The priests chanted back over the story of their nation's history, bringing it in remembrance before God. They led the people in repenting of their own sins. Then they confessed the iniquities of their fathers. (Nehemiah 9:2)

Later, the leaders entered into a sealed agreement with the LORD God Jehovah. Johanan remembered the solemnity of the moment. The commitment to follow God's law was so deep.

"Pretty deep in thought!" The words jolted Johanan back to

reality. He became aware that Havilah was standing beside him, but he hadn't even noticed her approach. He turned to see who had spoken.

The elderly Nehemiah dismounted his horse and came over to Johanan. Together they stood looking down on the city scene, the singing, the dancing, and the worship. Nehemiah was silent for a while. Then he turned to Johanan.

"Are you remembering . . ." his voice trailed off. Their eyes locked. Johanan's were filled with tears.

"Repentance," he murmured.

"Yes." Nehemiah paused as if for emphasis. "How can we help the people see that repentance is the foundation of forward motion with our God?"

Havilah came over and took Johanan's arm. Together they looked out over the scene.

Without a vision, there would be no return.
Without a return, there would be no worship.
Without worship, there would be no repentance.
Without repentance, there would be no temple.
Without a temple, there would be no walls.
Without walls, the city had no validity.
Without validity, there would be no dominion.

* * * *

Here I sit, thousands of years later, with the same question. How do I convince the people of God that efforts at dominion, walls, or temples are hopeless without repentance?

> **For behold this selfsame thing, that ye sorrowed after a godly sort, what carefulness it wrought in you, yea, what clearing of yourselves, yea, what indignation, yea, what fear, yea, what vehement desire, yea, what zeal, yea, what revenge! In all things ye have approved yourselves to be clear in this matter. (2 Corinthians 7:11)**

Paul, in writing to the Corinthians the second time, reminded them of their experience of his first letter. It had brought great sorrow to them. The sorrow, then, had brought them to a place of deep, godly repentance. In that repentance, a change took place that produced a wholeness which forbade their going back again.

The deep sorrow brought carefulness—a combing through life to identify violations.

The carefulness brought clearing, or apology.

The clearing brought indignation—being vexed that they were affected by the past.

The indignation brought fear—a sense of sobriety about what else might be troubling them.

The fear brought vehement desire.

The vehement desire morphed into zeal.

The zeal brought about revenge—a desire for vengeance against evil.

At the end, there was a clearness and a sense of motivation that had not been there before they received Paul's letter. Therefore, Paul was rejoicing, not for all the sorrow and tears, but for wholeness and clarity.

The people of God in Nehemiah's day also lacked clarity. They were returning to Jerusalem, yet walking as if in a fog. They did not seem to have clarity even in things like relating to enemies such as Tobiah. The return to Jerusalem was good. The beginning of the daily sacrifices was wonderful. Even the thought of rebuilding the temple was admirable.

The problem, the major holdup in this scene, was one of alignment with God's law. Misalignment with that law brought people into a place of murkiness. God had brought severe punishment in the form of exile, with great suffering and loss. Now He was bringing them back... but they needed realignment.

Ezra stood on a large wooden pulpit and read the law. The first element in godly repentance is hearing what GOD says. Ezra read the Book of the Law. John the Baptist was the voice in the wilderness, turning the hearts of the fathers to the children and calling for repentance. Jesus urged people to repent because the kingdom of heaven was at hand. In Acts 2, the people heard the word of God from Peter, and were "pricked in their hearts." Paul heard a voice from heaven, and he repented. He later wrote to the Corinthians, sparking their own repentance.

If we cannot hear what God wants or is saying, there is nothing to come in line with. We humans have a huge propensity to compare ourselves with others and come into line with that rather than with God.

> **For we dare not make ourselves of the number, or compare ourselves with some that commend themselves: but they measuring themselves by themselves, and comparing themselves among themselves, are not wise. (2 Corinthians 10:12)**

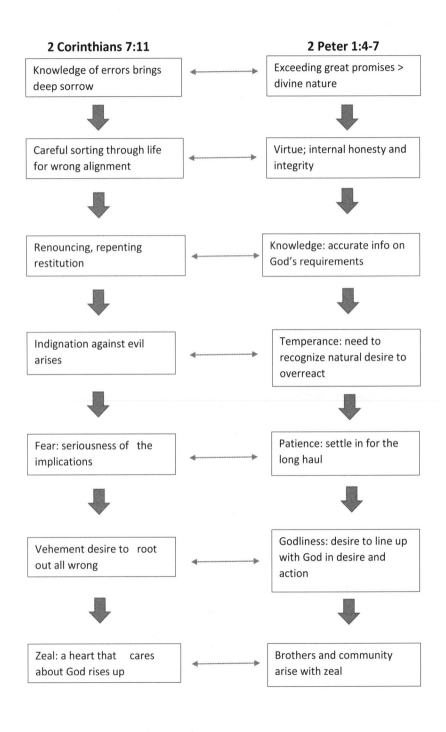

The primary role of a prophet is to help people see what they need to come into alignment with. Nehemiah called Ezra a prophet. Jesus called John a prophet. The people called Jesus a prophet. People understood, at least vaguely, the need to have someone who could help identify where the misalignments with God actually lay. Paul said this calling of prophet is part of the foundation of the church.

Generally, though, people have not particularly appreciated the idea of prophets. Jeremiah wept and pled with the people of God BEFORE the judgment fell. They threw him in a pit. Stephen noted that prophets were generally disrespected and killed. He too, was put to death for his observations. 1,500 years later, Felix Manz joined those ranks.

The Law of God, and the realities of Christ and His Kingdom, demand an adherence. Either we come into alignment with it, or it grinds us to powder.

And whosoever shall fall on this stone shall be broken: but on whomsoever it shall fall, it will grind him to powder. (Matthew 21:44)

The question facing Western Christians today is, will we hear Gods way and come into alignment and repent? Or will we join the ranks of those who compare, jeer, and mock the prophets and God's law? I hear much today that reminds me of Nehemiah's day. Think about the parallels:

- If we are just saved, isn't that enough?
- If we just build a temple, isn't that enough?
- There is no way to go back over my life righting wrong.

- There is no way to build this wall again.
- Surely God doesn't expect people to look like weirdos.
- God doesn't mind a little mixing with pagan spouses.

Somewhere, there must be a clear reading of what God says and wants, followed by sincere sorrow of heart.

Our free elections and democratic systems of government in the West have ushered in much peace and freedom. However, they have also colored our theology in an unhealthy way. The kingdom Jesus preached is a KINGDOM, not a democracy. This KINGDOM has a KING, and He writes the LAW. Our reality is to come in line with His decrees without question, debate, vote, or consensus.

When Christ speaks, He speaks as LORD. Anything we do against what He says is kicking against the pricks. (Acts 9:5) Jesus likened disobedience to building a house on the sand. Note that the house could indeed be built; it just had no safety in the storm and no future except destruction. (Matthew 7:24-27)

Jesus was also very clear that rank and ability in the kingdom would be predicated on His law and our attitude toward it.

Whosoever therefore shall break one of these least commandments, and shall teach men so, he shall be called the least in the kingdom of heaven: but whosoever shall do and teach them, the same shall be called great in the kingdom of heaven. (Matthew 5:19)

It is way past time for us to humble ourselves, put on sackcloth, and read what is written. It is time for God's people to determine to line up with His TRUTH, regardless of cost. May repentance once again be treasured and sought.

The second element that needs to occur is a "causing to understand." (Nehemiah 8:8) People are not likely to comprehend what God wants unless they are taught or caused to understand. Ezra knew this, and he surrounded himself with folks who could help give the sense of what was read. The reality, the point-blank clarity of divine holiness must not be softened in an effort to appease the masses.

There is no special virtue in being offensive; but then, neither is there any virtue in softening the blow that comes when Christ confronts culture. Efforts to blunt the sword of the Word of God don't result in a blunted sword. Rather, they result in an absence of the sword altogether. This sword was meant to pierce, and pierce it shall. Piercing of the sword of the Spirit never implies comfort. Neither does the concept of repentance. (Hebrews 4:12)

From heaven's kingdom perspective, it is all fairly simple. When people hear God's Word and choose to repent, God feels welcome. The great revivals and moves of God—whether in our story here, in John the Baptist's ministry, in Acts 19, or in modern times—are all marked by serious repentance. When the reading of His Word is bent and twisted to coddle current cultural trends, or if it is discontinued and God is not welcome there, He leaves. We either fall on the rock, or it falls on us.

Scripture prophesied that before Jesus was revealed, there would be a voice crying in the wilderness. (Isaiah 40:3-5) This voice would cry for the crooked to be straightened and the rough smoothed. When John the Baptist came, his message was to repent. The reason for it? The kingdom of heaven was close by.

This reality is not simply a plan or a historical event. It is a pattern—a spiritual law of foundations. God calls us to repent, and THEN the kingdom becomes a reality before us. Even within the kingdom, advancement is predicated on repentance.

The message of repentance is not one of hate or anger. It is a message of hope, love, and clarity! God calls us to repent, to align ourselves with His channels of blessings. Ezra knew that the people were out of line with God's law, and so they would continually be in turmoil, trouble, heartache, and devastation. He caused them to understand God's law in order to bring about their realignment with it. This realignment then could bring a season of restoration, revival, and blessing.

So what is repentance? Repentance is a change in direction. This comes about by a change of mind. Since the mind is directed by the heart more than by information, repentance is generally characterized by a sincere change of heart. So it works like this:

Heart change → Mind change → Direction change

Many times, when someone shows emotion (tears) folks assume the heart has changed. However, wisdom and experience will want to see DIRECTION change. If there is no change of direction, there may have indeed been a sorrow, but it was the sorrow of the world. (2 Corinthians 7:10)

Repentance—real, genuine repentance with a change of heart—is a gift from heaven. A man can "make up his mind," and some personalities are especially good at it. But regardless of determination levels and willpower, a man can no more change his own heart than a leopard can change his spots.

Can the Ethiopian change his skin, or the leopard his spots? then may ye also do good, that are accustomed to do evil. (Jeremiah 13:23)

Man cannot change himself. Many men, especially young,

strong men (and some women) believe they can. This is foolishness. If we could simply determine to do right and do it, we would have no need of Christ. If right living or right standing with God could have come by a law, it would have by now.

Is the law then against the promises of God? God forbid: for if there had been a law given which could have given life, verily righteousness should have been by the law. (Galatians 3:21)

Repentance deals with far more than a list of behaviors. It extends into the very desire of the "want-er" within man, the heart. Peter says that "of whom a man is overcome, of the same is he brought in bondage." (2 Peter 2:19) Paul says "his servants you are, to whom you obey." (Romans 6:16) Jesus regarded mammon as a master to those caught in its grip. (Luke 16:13) Each of these perspectives portrays the drive in the heart as a person. While the argument could be made that each is using pictorial language, the element of bondage is clear.

People do what people do because of what they feel.

If we are going to be able to change, it must be through the gift of repentance. Only through repentance does the nature and WANT of the heart change. If we are to help others change and change direction, we must help them repent, for only by repentance do the feelings of the heart change.

Repentance is a gift. Like most of God's gifts to man, it is a gift readily given, but it requires a specific POSTURE to receive.

Ezra and Nehemiah prepared the people for a posture. The reading of the Law of Moses brought great conviction, but they knew the posture was not correct. Therefore, they instigated a day of rejoicing to bring about corrected posture. This was followed by a week of simple obedience and deep mourning of repentance.

This needs to include a sense of corporate care for one another. (Nehemiah 8:10) This rejoicing and caring for others is an important part of foundational repentance in kingdom economy.

Then there was preparation. Three weeks later, folks showed up in correct posture, ready to hear and to receive repentance. They sat in sackcloth with ashes and earth on their heads, prepared to mourn, weep, and experience the agony of an eternal God changing hearts in time.

Most of us have viewed repentance through a very wrong lens. We remember the tearing inside, the pain, the humiliation, the tears, the snot, and the wailing. But we forget so quickly the sweetness of new alignment with the Holy Spirit of Christ.

I would say, rejoice! I want to see folks stumbling up the old sawdust trail, blinded by their tears but with hands raised in both surrender and praise because they get to repent again. That conviction of error and sin by the Spirit should be sought after, for it is a GIFT from heaven. Tip: never say no to gifts from heaven!

And the servant of the Lord must not strive; but be gentle unto all men, apt to teach, patient, In meekness instructing those that oppose themselves; if God peradventure will give them repentance to the acknowledging of the truth; And that they may recover themselves out of the snare of the devil, who are taken captive by him at his will. (2 Timothy 2:24-26)

God is always right. We are not. Our posture as Christ-followers needs to be one of "poor in spirit." We sit constantly in a posture of repentance before Him, inviting Him to change us continually into His likeness. This posture does not need to conflict in any way with the confidence of our position in Christ, or with the powerful authority He calls us to walk in.

Repentance is what uncovers the foundations we need in order to build a wall. Sanballats and Tobiahs will fight repentance as if they were on steroids. Entire denominations have removed both the concept and the word *repentance* from their theology altogether. These are the ones who have chosen friendship with Tobiah over a walk with God. That salt has lost its flavor.

This process or this lifestyle of repentance so angers the demonic world that there will be a fight. It is difficult to have a solid fighting stance against evil, and yet a pliable, surrendered heart toward God. Digging through the things we have believed toward a repentance that uncovers foundations requires a level of personal honesty that many cannot accept. One must muscle past the fear, the exposure, and the vulnerability to a place where the promise of repentance and change ranks higher than the possibility of rejection and pain.

Only here in this vulnerable place can we build with one hand while we hold a spear in the other. Only here can foundations be uncovered.

But don't let your strength decay.

There is much rubbish.

Q. Why has the notion of repentance fallen into disrepute?

Q. How would you explain the "conflict" between a heart of repentance and a confidence and joy in our position and gifting in Christ?

Q. Honesty invites repentance. In what area have you allowed dishonesty to take root?

> Man was made for dominion, by God Himself; Much of the evil in the world, is a misdirection of that God-breathed desire. -SS

CHAPTER 11

Dominion

Johanan leaned back in his seat and surveyed the happy scene before him. He gave Havilah a squeeze, and she smiled at him. Taking a sip of wine from the goblet he held, he returned her smile.

It was the second day of the wedding celebration for their oldest son. Havilah was ecstatic at the choice he had made, and of course, so was their son! Children shouted and danced nearby. Neighbors kept dropping by to offer good wishes and blessings to the lovestruck couple. Gifts were piling up in the next room. Many guests, including some of the rulers of the city, had dropped by. More would be coming to celebrate and enjoy the dinner feast after the evening sacrifice.

A commotion in the direction of the city gate caught Johanan's ear. He got up and walked that direction, trying to see what was happening. Judging by the crowds gathering near the gate, something of note seemed to be happening. Apparently, it was something good because the shouting sounded joyful.

Wait! Was that Nehemiah? The camel knelt, and an old, white-bearded man awkwardly dismounted. He had returned from Shushan the palace for the last time. Johanan was elated to see him again.

Of course, Nehemiah came over to join in the joyous celebration. Youngsters plied him with questions, and the kindly old man obliged with story after story. He described palaces and cities, lands and rivers, journeys and bands of robbers. And always, he wove into the stories the greatness and faithfulness of Jehovah.

Later in the night, as they poked the fire embers, Nehemiah asked Johanan about the local state of affairs. Then they retired to their rooms. Still, Johanan had the niggling sense that something was amiss.

They attended the morning sacrifice together the next day. Johanan did much of the actual work now, even though his father Eliashib was the high priest in charge. That mantle would fall on Johanan in several years.

Nehemiah may have been aging, but Johanan realized that he was still sharp. His gait was strong, his eyes were steely, and his gaze was fierce. There was something of smoke in the eyes though . . . something unspoken.

Johanan returned to the house and greeted his wife. Their conversation about the day's plans was interrupted by a sudden ruckus near the temple. Considering this to be his personal area of responsibility, Johanan ran toward the commotion.

It was caused by Nehemiah. He had an axe. Amidst the shouts of exclamation, horror, and general din, Johanan surveyed the scene. Nehemiah was completely focused on his task. Ignoring the yells, he swung the ax again and again, chopping the couch in half. Then he hoisted the half piece on his shoulder, carried it down the street to the wall, and dumped it unceremoniously over the wall.

He came back for the other half and repeated the process, ignoring the crowds as if they did not exist. Then he entered the temple and returned dragging a table. He was in the process of axing it when Eliashib came puffing up the temple hill.

Nehemiah paused. He laid down the ax and approached Eliashib. The crowd went silent with tense expectation.

"You!" Nehemiah spat vehemently. "You let this enemy of God into the temple. NO MORE!"

Father Eliashib hung his head. Johanan put his hand on his father's shoulder, patted it briefly, and walked resolutely up to Nehemiah, who was back to his ax.

"Let me help," Johanan said.

He and Nehemiah worked all that morning. They took all of Tobiah's household goods and threw them out on a heap over the wall. That afternoon, they cleansed the room and brought the vessels of God back into it.

> **And I came to Jerusalem, and understood of the evil that Eliashib did for Tobiah, in preparing him a chamber in the courts of the house of God. And it grieved me sore: therefore I cast forth all the household stuff to Tobiah out of the chamber. Then I commanded, and they cleansed the chambers: and thither brought I again the vessels of the house of God, with the meat offering and the frankincense. (Nehemiah 13:7-9)**

As they worked, Nehemiah kept muttering under his breath, but Johanan caught only the word "dominion." He understood better when the city elders came for a meeting later that day. Nehemiah lit them up with his fearless rebukes.

"Where are the singers? Where is the praise and the music? Why hasn't this place been cleaned?" Nehemiah demanded.

In the end, Nehemiah set Shelemiah in charge of the treasury. The rulers brought in money and offerings. Praise once again sounded from the temple, and every detail was attended to by the Levites. People began to pour in again from the countryside to worship and pray. They brought offerings, and Johanna was shocked at the abundance.

"Dominion," muttered Nehemiah.

But the old man's rampage wasn't finished. When he saw people bringing in loads of fruit and produce on the Sabbath, he called a city meeting. There he dressed down the nobles of the city, scolding as only an old Jewish prophet can.

"Haven't we been in bondage long enough?" he thundered. "God brought evil on us for this behavior, and would you repeat it?"

Then I contended with the nobles of Judah, and said unto them, What evil thing is this that ye do, and profane the sabbath day? Did not your fathers thus, and did not our God bring all this evil upon us, and upon this city? yet ye bring more wrath upon Israel by profaning the sabbath. (Nehemiah 13:17, 18)

On the eve of the next Sabbath, Nehemiah took Johanan to the gates of the city.

"Shut and lock them," Nehemiah instructed.

Even as Johanan helped do just that, he knew the custom was for the next day to be market day. But early the following morning, even before sunrise, Nehemiah knocked impatiently at the door. Johanan followed him once more to the gates.

Johanan saw Nehemiah's guards already standing by the gate. Nehemiah seemed to go electric. Standing on the wall and looking down on the market vendors, the old man raised his voice to a shout.

"GO HOME!" he bellowed. "This is the Sabbath. We do NO MARKET on the Sabbath of God from now on."

The marketgoers seemed confused. They even camped out at the gates a time or two, but then Nehemiah told them in no uncertain terms that if they came again, he would kill them.

And it came to pass, that when the gates of Jerusalem began to be dark before the sabbath, I commanded that the gates should be shut, and charged that they should not be opened till after the sabbath: and some of my servants set I at the gates, that there should no burden be brought in on the sabbath day. So the merchants and sellers of all kind of ware lodged without Jerusalem once or twice. Then I testified against them, and said unto them, "Why lodge ye about the wall? if ye do so again, I will lay hands on you." From that time forth came they no more on the sabbath. (Nehemiah 13:19-21)

That seemed to get through to them.

Standing there on the wall, Nehemiah turned to Johanan and locked his steel gaze on him. Johanan waited.

"My son," Nehemiah said, "we don't take orders. We give orders. It is called DOMINION. Never, in God's plan, did He ordain for

His people to learn from godless cultures or to take orders from them. YOU hear from God, and YOU give THEM orders."

Johanan realized later that it took a while to soak in. The next day, when he saw the white-haired Nehemiah chasing someone through the temple courts, shouting and shaking his staff, it was clearer. Especially when Johanan realized it was his own nephew that Nehemiah was chasing out of the city.

> **And one of the sons of Joiada, the son of Eliashib the high priest, was son in law to Sanballat the Horonite: therefore I chased him from me. (Nehemiah 13:28)**

The son of Johanan's brother Joiada had married a daughter of Judah's enemy, Sanballat. Nehemiah chased him out of the temple. This brought quite a stir and ended with a huge city meeting. Nehemiah was livid, smacking folks with his staff and even pulling some of their hair out.

"DOMINION!" He shouted. He had them all swear not to repeat this evil of failure to separate again.

Johanan lived many years in Jerusalem with his wife Havilah and their sons. He watched his grandsons grow up, and he gave his daughters away to fine young men.

But long after Nehemiah had died and was buried with his fathers, that concept kept ringing in Johanan's head.

Dominion.

So THAT was what Zerubbabel and Jeshua saw all those years ago. THAT was what drove old Prophet Ezra and his friend Nehemiah. The recent scroll by Ezra from the visions of Zechariah also came into focus.

The God Who called them His people, the God of Abraham, Isaac and Jacob, was Jehovah alone. He intended His people to be His representatives on earth. All yokes with the Sanballats and the Tobiahs had to be broken so that the people might follow the Lord in dominion.

Johanan walked off the pages of our Bible into the mist of the past, and we shall let him slip off the pages of this book too. But you ... you still live.

If you are reading this, I am assuming that you have left Babylon, or at least that you wish to. Have you completed the temple yet? There is much to be done. Have you uncovered the foundations?

What about the daily sacrifice? Has it been established in your life and your family? Are the walls of your life raised high, giving safety to all within the gates? Has Tobiah's stuff been cleaned out of the temple?

Are you walking in dominion?

Those who lived in Nehemiah's day saw neither the need for nor the significance of the walls. But the enemy did.

Sanballat and Tobiah reacted in extreme ways when the wall was being built. Why anyone would rent them a room in the temple still baffles me. They were obviously enemies of the people of God. Yet somehow, they gained access to the very center of worship. Their voices were heard echoing in the temple where only the voices of praise and the truth should have been.

This travesty in worship could not be halted until the WALL was built. That required digging for the foundations. And there was much rubbish. That rubbish had to be removed before they could erect a solid wall. The walls and gates gave the city dominion, and they will give you dominion as well.

Sanballat and Tobiah represent the demonic world and the godless culture it produces. When your city is built and finished, you rule. No more taking orders from culture and society. You may live around and among it all, but there will be no alliances built. When there is confrontation with the dark side, there will be much fear . . . on their side. You, by contrast, will walk in confidence of the blood of the Lamb.

Fear is not part of your inheritance as a follower of Jehovah. He has not given you a spirit of fear, but of power, love, and a sound mind. It isn't so much that we are commanded not to fear (although we are.) It is simply that a walled city with locked gates has no reason to fear.

The three friends of Daniel found this courage before Nebuchadnezzar. They saw no reason to even exercise carefulness in it.

Shadrach, Meshach, and Abednego, answered and said to the king, O Nebuchadnezzar, we are not careful to answer thee in this matter. If it be so, our God whom we serve is able to deliver us from the burning fiery furnace, and he will deliver us out of thine hand, O king. But if not, be it known unto thee, O king, that we will not serve thy gods, nor worship the golden image which thou hast set up. (Daniel 3:16-18)

Their confidence was not in themselves, but in the reality of their God's deliverance. Their decision was final, king or no king, and their allegiance was fixed. Idolatry was not an option.

Extreme emotion seized the (enemy) king. He lost the mightiest men in his army that day, and he also lost face. His idols and gods lost credibility and dominion. The only thing Daniel's three friends lost was the rope that had bound them.

This type of dominion is not given to everyone. It is a result of the determination not to defile one's self with the king's meat. Daniel built the wall around his own life very carefully and purposefully, and so did his friends.

> **But Daniel purposed in his heart that he would not defile himself with the portion of the king's meat, nor with the wine which he drank: therefore he requested of the prince of the eunuchs that he might not defile himself. (Daniel 1:8)**

He refused to do what seemed expedient in favor of what was superlative. This refusal to compromise even a little, at the threat of life itself, allowed Daniel and his friends to be used multiple times as agents of heaven. "Thy kingdom come, Thy will be done on earth," is an idle cry if it comes from someone defiled by the king's meat. God's name was hallowed by these men, and even the enemy king declared Him worthy of honor.

> **Therefore I make a decree, That every people, nation, and language, which speak anything amiss against the God of Shadrach, Meshach, and Abednego, shall be cut in pieces, and their houses shall be made a dunghill: because there is no other God that can deliver after this sort. (Daniel 3:29)**

Many of us today wish for these moves of God in our nations and areas of influence. Yet, who among us can say with Jesus, "And for their sakes I sanctify myself, that they also might be sanctified through the truth."? (John 17:19) We want to have dominion over evil and have the power of the resurrection without the reality of the cross.

The brilliance of heaven shone on Daniel's demeanor. Heaven's wisdom found an outlet and a spokesperson on earth through him. That wisdom flowed from the throne of God unabridged, and the most powerful king in the world at that time fell down and worshipped this DOMINION of heaven in Daniel.

> **Then the king Nebuchadnezzar fell upon his face, and worshipped Daniel, and commanded that they should offer an oblation and sweet odours unto him. The king answered unto Daniel, and said, Of a truth it is, that your God is a God of gods, and a Lord of kings, and a revealer of secrets, seeing thou couldest reveal this secret. (Daniel 2:46, 47)**

However, all of this FOLLOWED Daniel's building of personal wall in his life and his refusal to be defiled.

Heaven still waits. The eyes of the Lord run to and fro throughout the earth, seeking opportunity to show Himself strong for those with perfect hearts. (2 Chronicles 16:9) God still seeks a man to stand in the gap (Ezekiel 22:30) to halt or slow impending destruction. The Spirit of Christ seeks to exert His mighty power and dominion through us—but alas, the very concept of HOLY has fallen into disrepute. The notion of dominion has been so warped by selfish men that heaven doesn't even recognize it. The pursuit of power outside the concept of HOLY is a dangerous, evil, and deadly game.

Your life was meant for dominion.

Your life needs a center of worship, a temple. The altar of your spirit should have a sacrifice of praise and of surrender continually. Then comes the building of the wall. This building requires the removal of massive amounts of rubbish from the past to uncover the foundations of Christ. There is much rubbish. Sorting through it all is tiring.

And then there are the attacks. The Sanballats and Tobiahs of your life: the lust, the anger, the fear, the witchcraft, the bitterness, the accusation, the jealousy, the unbelief, and the immorality attack continually. They know. They understand exactly what will happen if you are allowed to finish building your wall. You may not fully comprehend dominion, but they do. They and all their friends from hell shudder at the very notion of your life lived in dominion.

These agents from hell will fight your building of a temple. They do not like when folks get born again, and they resist it. Still, that alone is not a serious threat to THEIR dominion. They can always just rent a room in the temple. They can speak there, and the voices heard echoing in the chambers and hallways of the temple will not lead to dominion or clarity.

Tobiah will make all the alliances he can in the city of your life. He knows. He fears the day you might build a wall. He hates the concept of repentance and fights every hint of it. He does all in his power to fight against any consciousness of HOLY. He perverts the meaning and concept of holiness and rightness of life, which were meant to be walls of defense in our lives. He has succeeded in most of our Western Christianity, to the point that any attempt at righteous living is openly mocked and derided.

"Judge not!" has become the war cry of Sanballat as he fights the building of any wall. Most temple builders have decided to simply make friends with these enemies of God. It brings instant peace, no doubt, but the unseen cost is a releasing of dominion to the Sanballats and Tobiahs of our lives.

> **Nevertheless the foundation of God standeth sure, having this seal, The Lord knoweth them that are his. And, let everyone that nameth the name of Christ depart from iniquity. But in a great house there are not only vessels of gold and of silver, but also of wood and of earth; and some to honor, and some to dishonor. If a man therefore purge himself from these, he shall be a vessel unto honor, sanctified, and meet for the master's use, and prepared unto every good work. (2 Timothy 2:19-21)**

Vessels of honor are held in the hands of the King. His dominion flows through them, and of the increase of His government there shall be no end. May His kingdom come, may His will be done on earth as it is in heaven, and may His name be hallowed.

Journey to Effective Kingdom Authority

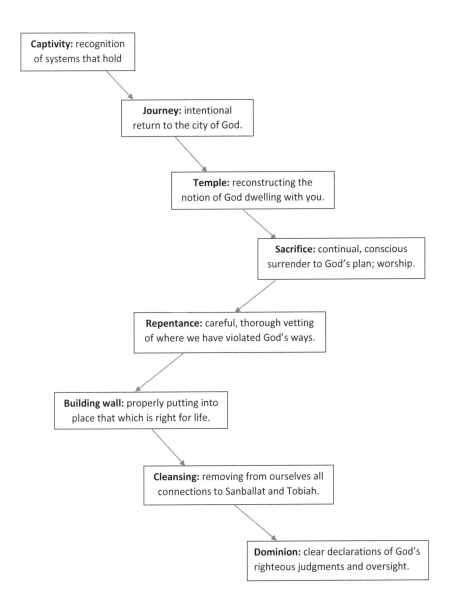

Q. Define the notion of dominion in your own terms.

_____
_____
_____
_____
_____

Q. When there was no temple, things seemed peaceful. It was only when the temple came, and later the wall, that serious conflict occurred. What made this conflict necessary?

_____
_____
_____
_____
_____

Q. Are there things in your life owned by some Sanballat or Tobiah that keep you from building a wall? What area do you seek dominion in?

_____
_____
_____
_____
_____

> Jerusalem, City of Peace, where Christ is King, Light, and Saviour. -SS

CHAPTER 12

Jerusalem

Jerusalem represents the city of peace and the city of God. In the beginning, God saw all that He had made, and it was good. Very good. All of creation was synced in one great harmony. Food was abundant, healthy, complete, and pleasant. Adam and Eve were to have dominion over every living plant and animal, which were all vegetarians. All Adam had to do was transplant flowers and bushes daily as Eve desired.

> **And God blessed them, and God said unto them, Be fruitful, and multiply, and replenish the earth, and subdue it: and have dominion over the fish of the sea, and over the fowl of the air, and over every living thing that moveth upon the earth. (Genesis 1:28)**

God as King, Supreme Ruler, Creator, Life, Love, and Judge, created as Creator. Everything came out of Him by His Word. It was all good as He is good. It was perfect, orderly, defined, life, and peace.

Adam stooped down to move a tulip to another location. His cell phone lay on the ground beside him. He glanced at his watch and retied the laces on his sneakers, admiring the elastic rubber insoles. Then he paused for a hot swig of coffee from the insulated mug on his belt.

Perhaps reading the above paragraph makes you wonder about my sanity. After all, NONE of those things existed for Adam.

True enough, but here is my point: the SCIENCE, the LAWS all these things operate by, already existed in Eden.

God created. God created order. Into that order were written laws. Hundreds and even thousands of laws crisscrossed the universe in absolute perfection. Greater laws overrode lesser ones. No laws clashed. Every star and planet hummed in perfect harmony with every flower. There was no offbeat and no dissonance. The lion lay by the lamb, and everything breathed in congruence and perfect synchronization.

The laws governing math, music, and science shot like lasers across the sky. Every law of right and of microbiology cut clear pathways through the earth. Creation was paradise.

But there was one TREE . . .

God rested. The Creator of heaven and earth lay back in His hammock of perfectly woven, absolutely correct laws, and He rested.

There is no indication of how long this time of bliss lasted. We do know that no death occurred during this time. And we also know that one day, sin came.

Eve believed the serpent and took a bite. Adam took a bite also.

A resounding, screeching howl tore through the bushes and plants. It dented the trees, tore through the water, and flashed out into the universe. It reverberated from planet to star, tearing at the laser laws, finally sucking itself into endless black holes in space. It was the ultimate dissonance, the clash of anti-law, the offbeat of SIN.

Creation wilted. Violated, torn laws manifested themselves in thorny bushes and thistles. The earth revolted. Emotions and thoughts, violations of creation itself, surged forward in Adam and Eve.

Adam was ashamed.

He blamed Eve.

Eve blamed the serpent.

The serpent didn't have a leg to stand on.

And all because of one tree, one choice. It was the tree of KNOWLEDGE. It was the tree of the knowledge of GOOD. It was the tree of the knowledge of good and EVIL. It was the fruit of that tree of violation of perfect law.

Wherefore, as by one man sin entered into the world, and death by sin; and so death passed upon all men, for that all have sinned ... (Romans 5:12)

Now, some years later, Adam raised his wooden hoe and struck the ground, chopping off a thistle in the lentil patch. Sweat ran off his face and itched under the skin garment he wore. Innocent blood had been shed to provide a skin to cover the shame of his sin. He glanced at his oldest son, not realizing he was seeing the world's first murderer.

His cell phone lay beside him on the ground, undiscovered. It would lie there for another 6,000 years before it was found. During all that time, the laws existed. Science CREATES nothing.

Rather, it is a discipline of discovery, discovering LAW that has existed since Adam first kissed Eve.

Gravity is a law that was there.

The basis for Einstein's theory of relativity was there.

Al-Khwarizmi's algebra was there.

Edison's light bulb was there.

Thousands upon thousands of laws crisscrossing the universe, placed in motion by the Creator of all, have yet to be discovered.

Science continues its discoveries at a rapid pace, aided by machines, computers, telescopes, and microscopes. Intricate laws governing the smallest cells are carefully studied and analyzed. Elements and atoms are listed and categorized to make more laws easily recognized. The electronic revolution of the past few decades has been absolutely astounding.

But somehow in the dash forward to the new, it is easy to forget or even despise the old. We quickly forget that the laws were put in place long ago, and there is nothing new under the sun. We are often tempted to discard the old and grab something new and different that we think might be better. Violating old laws doesn't make us progressive or smart; instead, it brings us into conflict with the One Who wrote the laws to begin with.

God's laws are placed into motion without regard for people's opinions. When a person once realizes that LAW operates outside of human influence, he is then ready to submit to it, discover it, and flow with it. This is why Peter says so aptly, **And if ye call on the Father, who without respect of persons judgeth according to every man's work, pass the time of your sojourning here in fear: (1 Peter 1:17)**

Some of these laws are spiritual.

All that is discovered in real science is simply law that already existed in Eden. However, as fascinated as we may be with science, math, and physics, there is an even greater reality. This reality has been better understood by people of other times. Today, it tends to be snubbed because of our obsession with the human mind and its "education." Science belongs in a realm where physical law can be established by observation, measurability, and reproduction.

But scripture is clear that the physical was made by the spiritual; therefore the spiritual is greater.

> **Through faith we understand that the worlds were framed by the word of God, so that things which are seen were not made of things which do appear. (Hebrews 11:3)**

Not much has been understood, at least in recent years, of spiritual LAW. In fact, the entire notion of spiritual law has become a byword. Much of this has arisen because of failed efforts to align with spiritual law by willpower alone.

If humanity would simply relax, lie on the grass, look at the stars, and THINK, they would begin to see quite a lot of spiritual law. Paul says in Romans 1 that these things are clearly seen.

> **Because that which may be known of God is manifest in them; for God hath shewed it unto them. For the invisible things of him from the creation of the world are clearly seen, being understood by the things that are made, even his eternal power and Godhead; so that they are without excuse. (Romans 1:19, 20)**

When man allows his own desires or selfishness to crowd out knowledge of spiritual law, he goes dark. Very dark. It's an old problem.

God delivered a written copy of moral law to Moses to help stymie the effects of the sonic boom of sin.

Wherefore then serveth the law? It was added because of transgressions, till the seed should come to whom the promise was made; and it was ordained by angels in the hand of a mediator. (Galatians 3:19)

People kept violating God's law written in the universe, so He wrote it in stone.

Man hurried to add to it, water it down, define it, and defy it. The cause-and-effect justice of the law, brought people into bondage repeatedly. Our entire book is the saga of a return from such bondage.

Then came Jesus, the ultimate plan, the Christ of heaven, innocent of breaking even the least of the laws. His perfect BLOOD covers my shame, the effect of my participation with that horrible fruit of sonic boom—SIN. His BLOOD balances the scale of justice in heaven, because it has no stain of sin in it. This scale is the justice of the Judge Who wrote all the law to begin with.

Keep in mind that the LAW was not arbitrary. It issued forth from the very character and nature of Christ. That is why Jesus never violated any of the laws, small or great. After all, He wrote them out of His own nature! And His lack of violation completely freed Him from the power of DEATH. He could lay down His life and take it back up again.

> **O death, where is thy sting? O grave, where is thy victory? The sting of death is sin; and the strength of sin is the law. But thanks be to God, which giveth us the victory through our Lord Jesus Christ. (1 Corinthians 15:55-57)**

Now if you understand somewhat of the reality and immutability of law written from heaven, let us move forward to kingdom.

Much of Jesus' teaching is about the kingdom. Kingdoms have kings, and kings make the law. Obedience to the eternal King and His laws brings blessing and makes the King happy. Dismissal of the King's laws is disrespectful, and is tantamount to treason.

When Jesus taught about prayer, He reiterated this line: "Thy kingdom come, thy will be done, on earth, as it is in heaven." This is intended to communicate several things:

- There is a kingdom.
- It needs to come here.
- There is a King.
- He has a will (order).
- That will is good and desirable.
- The law of kingdom is perfectly honored in heaven.
- We desire to see that law honored here.
- With that phrase, we state that we want to come in line with heaven's law.
- Violation of law always carries penalty.

As we noted earlier, these penalties follow the violation of law, regardless of knowledge or personage. One of the realities that hurt Israel over and over was their notion of superiority—the idea that somehow, they could violate law without consequence. This is a concept I hear repeatedly today among Christians, and it is just shy of insanity.

You can walk off the top of your garage roof while loudly declaring that you will violate the law of gravity, but you will not. Gravity law wins. You hurt. That's how it works, one hundred percent of the time.

There is something in man, still ringing from the discordant shrieking sonic boom of sin, that wants God's law to be wrong. Just once, we would like to prove it wrong. The reality is, though, that God's law is perfect. In fact, if you yield to it, it will mold your soul into cohesive alignment with God's rightness.

Or you can fight law, and hurt.

It's your choice.

> **The law of the Lord is perfect, converting the soul: the testimony of the Lord is sure, making wise the simple. The statutes of the Lord are right, rejoicing the heart: the commandment of the Lord is pure, enlightening the eyes ... More to be desired are they than gold, yea, than much fine gold: sweeter also than honey and the honeycomb. (Psalm 19:7, 8, 10)**

Jesus made all this relatively clear in the sermon on the mount.

> **Do not think that I have come to abolish the Law or the Prophets; I have not come to abolish them but to fulfill them. 18 For truly I tell you, until heaven and earth disappear, not the smallest letter, not the least stroke of a pen, will by any means disappear from the Law until everything is accomplished. 19 Therefore anyone who sets aside one of the least of these commands and teaches others accordingly will be called least in the kingdom of heaven, but whoever practices and teaches these commands will be called great in the kingdom of heaven. (Matthew 5:17-19 NIV)**

Jesus fulfilled every law. Every detail of God's law is perfect. If you want forward motion in the kingdom, figure out the laws and line up with them.

THE #1 ELEMENT OF SPIRITUAL WARFARE IS LIVING IN ALIGNMENT WITH GOD'S ETERNAL LAW.

When Jesus died and shed perfect blood, it paid for my sin on the justice scale of heaven. When He rose again, I rose with Him, and He put in ME the Spirit of Christ, the very Spirit Who wrote all the law. I find every facet of law written into the universe to be absolutely fascinating. Sometimes, if I am quiet long enough and listen to the Spirit within, I begin to remember the future.

Perhaps by now you are a bit bewildered by this chapter. Allow me to break it down more clearly.

- Breaking laws hurts us and ultimately lands us in Babylon, a system of men's ideas.
- We turn toward Jerusalem, and begin a long journey back toward worship.
- We arrive and begin to sacrifice.
- We start the laborious task of building a place of safety and agreement with God, a temple for Him to dwell in.
- We begin to understand repentance and the importance of coming into line with law.
- We come to realize our walls are damaged. The breaking of laws has left us unprotected. We must rebuild those walls, but THERE IS MUCH RUBBISH!
- We finally complete walls and come into alignment with God's laws. This gives us dominion over evil around us.
- Forward motion!

If Israel could have stopped repeating the mistakes of the past, great things might have happened. But alas, the cycle of defeat seemed to reinvent itself every few generations. This meant little was ever discovered of spiritual law.

Math was advanced because some basic laws were discovered, systematized, and taught to the next generation. This platform became their starting point, allowing them to discover more advanced law.

The same was true with medical knowledge.

The same was true with electrical circuitry.

The same was true with reading. Until, that is, some cocky,

God-hating folks decided they could reinvent law and do it their own way. Fail. Reading ability and comprehension has declined in the U.S. ever since this foolishness in the late 1980s.

The point is that the law needs to be understood, recognized, and respected. It doesn't change with culture. There are thousands of spiritual laws and realities waiting to be discovered, lying on the ground like the cell phone was by Adam, ignored. Scripture says all of creation is still groaning from the shrieking dissonance of sin, waiting for the manifestation of the sons of God and redemption. (Romans 8:19-23)

That ye may be blameless and harmless, the sons of God, without rebuke, in the midst of a crooked and perverse nation, among whom ye shine as lights in the world. (Philippians 2:15)

I believe God longs to see His people, followers of Christ, accomplish far more in the spiritual realms than we have ever dreamed. Instead of forward motion, though, we repeat the cycles of Israel over and over. We violate spiritual law, and back to Babylon we go. Then it takes another generation to make the trip back again. Some of course, get swallowed up by Babylon and never leave.

This is why I said earlier that the most important element of spiritual warfare is to live right. If you and I want spiritual authority, then by all means learn spiritual law and live accurately. Teach well to your children what you have learned, so that they might move forward into yet greater realities.

Go back across your life, carefully, one thing at a time. Identify the places where you violated God's law, whether written or not.

> This is the covenant that I will make with them after those days, saith the Lord, I will put my laws into their hearts, and in their minds will I write them. (Hebrews 10:16)

> **Which shew the work of the law written in their hearts, their conscience also bearing witness... (Romans 2:15a)**

Repent. Dig for the foundations of Christ, his nature and character, and then build up a wall of defense against evil.

The gum you stole...
The person you disrespected...
The shouting and cursing at your dad...
The girl you slept with...
The feeling of rejection you carry...
The porn you looked at...
The jealousy you felt toward her...
The fear you walk in...
The witchcraft you touched...

These are the broken-down sections of wall in your life. Sort through the rubbish carefully. Yes, it is tiring. It is also the pathway to victory, to dominion, and ultimately, to greater spiritual realities and authority. Hundreds of people groups in many nations languish in hopeless darkness waiting for someone who has enough knowledge of LAW and enough authority to set them free.

Your neighbors wait. Your culture waits. The whole world waits... and hell fumes. Hell trembles at the notion of a generation who would LIVE according to God's law, possess the authority, and walk boldly in it. To keep this from happening, hell offers myriad attractions and temptations to just a "little" violation of law.

"Everyone else is doing it," they said. And so, they lived powerlessly.

Feeling the empty powerlessness of religion that denies the power of God, folks grope and grab vehemently, seeking to find some element of power that would bring legitimacy. Delving into unknown realms and dimensions, they violate spiritual laws in flagrant disregard in pursuit of experiences that might make them feel powerful. We don't seem to realize that the desire for power itself is driven by our need to feel superior to others and by basic selfishness. Jesus told His own commissioned 70 to stop rejoicing in their power over the demons.

Notwithstanding in this rejoice not, that the spirits are subject unto you; but rather rejoice, because your names are written in heaven. (Luke 10:20)

Pursue power in wild abandon, if you will. Pursue it with enough focus, and it will likely come to you, but at what cost? Not all that glitters is gold. Not all that masquerades as power even belongs to disciples of Christ. What does belong to us is a radical apprehension of the cross. In this cross, this notion Jesus invites us into, is the wisdom and the power of God.

There are spiritual laws that govern even miracles. The notion of walking around defying known law while trying to operate in unknown is like trying to do trigonometry when you cannot yet add. Getting the math wrong will not destroy you permanently. However, defying spiritual law might bring permanent destruction.

The simplest realities of spiritual law are spelled out rather clearly. Jesus said that hearing His sayings and doing them was like building a house on the rock. Storms will come, winds will blow, Sanballat and Tobiah will attack, but the house will stand.

Not DOING ... not aligning our life with the laws He spoke with the universe, is a calculated and invited disaster.

The Jerusalem of your life is to be a city of peace. It was designed to be a city set on a hill, giving light to all around it. Lives lined up with law find harmony everywhere. Fulfilled husbands speak love and tenderness to happy wives. Serene children jump and play and work and learn. Laughter rings. The earth itself yields her strength, while bees pollinate the trees. Contented cows graze the pastures, and milk and honey flows.

The whole neighborhood knows. Everyone watches in amazement as God's law is honored and blessing flows. There is, perhaps, no higher calling than this farmer and his wife have found: to honor God in all and to live in alignment with the laws of His universe.

Jerusalem. City of God. Your life, too, can be a place of safety and life. But at first, the walls must be built up. Don't be discouraged either by the attacks or by the sheer volume of work. Certainly, THERE IS MUCH RUBBISH.

But there is dominion ahead.

According to spiritual law, there needs to be a daily sacrifice before there can be a temple.

> **He that is faithful in that which is least is faithful also in much: and he that is unjust in the least is unjust also in much. (Luke 16:10)**

Kingdom principle, law, demands that we be faithful in the small before the big. The daily sacrifice in our lives is the site of temple foundation.

In spiritual law, being born again and building a temple in our own lives, is not an END in itself, but a means to an end. Jesus pointed to new faith as an entry point to kingdom reality, not its end. And He gently chided Nicodemus for not getting it.

> **Jesus answered, "Verily, verily, I say unto thee, except a man be born of water and of the Spirit, he cannot enter into the kingdom of God ... Marvel not that I said unto thee, 'Ye must be born again.'" Jesus answered and said unto him, "Art thou a master of Israel, and knowest not these things?" (John 3:5, 7, 10)**

What hell fears most and reacts most strongly to is someone getting a hold of spiritual law in the kingdom and using it. Jesus did it perfectly, and hell had no answer. Demons reacted and shook when He came around. Jesus said that the prince of this world had no access to Him.

> **Hereafter I will not talk much with you: for the prince of this world cometh, and hath nothing in me. (John 14:30)**

Paul points out that we wrestle against principalities and powers.

> **Put on the whole armour of God, that ye may be able to stand against the wiles of the devil. For we wrestle not against flesh and blood, but against principalities, against powers, against the rulers of the darkness of this world, against spiritual wickedness in high places. Wherefore take unto you the whole armour of God, that ye may be able to withstand in the evil day, and having done all, to stand. Stand therefore, having your loins girt about with truth, and having on the breastplate of righteousness; And your feet shod with the preparation of the gospel of peace; Above all, taking the shield of faith, wherewith ye shall be able to quench all the fiery darts of the wicked. And take the helmet of salvation, and the sword of the Spirit, which is the word of God: Praying always with all prayer and supplication in the Spirit, and watching thereunto with all perseverance and supplication for all saints. (Ephesians 6:11-18)**

To be effective in that fight, there must be a protection in place of alignment with law. (verse 14) Failure here leaves us exposed in the most vital of areas.

In our story, Johanan learned a great spiritual law. Let it not be lost on you. Nehemiah wept to see this law noticed, respected, and instigated. That spiritual law is the heartbeat of this entire book:

In order to operate in dominion, the walls and gates must be built.

Of course, it is very hard. It takes much work; it is slow, tedious, painful and tiring. But you are more than conquerors, so press on... even though there is much rubbish.

There remaineth therefore a rest unto the people of God. Let us therefore fear, lest, a promise being left us of entering into his rest, any of you should seem to come short of it. (Hebrews 4:9, 1)

Q. What remains to be done in building Jerusalem, City of Peace, in your life?

_____
_____
_____
_____
_____